Indian Resi...

Wawahte

The Northern Lights are Spirit Angels
that lift us to our feet when our wings have
trouble remembering how to fly

As told to **Robert P. Wells**
By Indian Residential School Survivors

ISBN: 978-1-4669-1717-0 (sc)
ISBN: 978-1-4669-1719-4 (hc)
ISBN: 978-1-4669-1718-7 (e)

Library of Congress Control Number: 2012903219

Trafford rev. 02/26/2013

Trafford
PUBLISHING® www.trafford.com

North America & international
toll-free: 1 888 232 4444 (USA & Canada)
phone: 250 383 6864 ♦ fax: 812 355 4082

Also by Robert P. Wells:

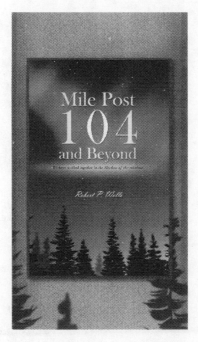

Mile Post 104 and Beyond

We have walked together in the Shadow of the rainbow

Robert P. Wells

Available now from Trafford Publishing by visiting www.trafford.com
You can order this title at your local bookseller or preferred on-line retailer.
978-1-4269-5796-3 (SC ISBN)
978-1-4269-5797-0 (HC ISBN)

C. 2

Dedication

A memorial to the children taken

and

the families left behind.

Wawahte is testimony to the strength of

the

Human Heart

TABLE OF CONTENTS

Acknowledgements

I t is customary at this point for the author to state he could not have done it without the usual list of contributors, family, and friends. This statement could not be more—true and my list is long—thank you.

In writing the historical narrative about the churches, Hudson's Bay Company, and Indian residential schools my first acknowledgement and credit goes to *The Beaver Magazine*, which was re-named *Canada's History Magazine* in 2010. I have throughout this book, drawn on but not specifically credited, some well-remembered ideas and words from long-forgotten issues of *The Beaver* to put Esther, Bunnie, and Stanley words into context and perspective. I extend my sincere appreciation to present and past staff and authors of this great Canadian icon.

I gratefully acknowledge Esther Faries (Love), Stanley Stephens, and Bunnie Galvin (Kries-Tenniscoe) for sharing their stories. I extend my thanks and appreciation to them. Special acknowledgments go to Chief Robert Joseph, Angela

White, and the other people of the British Columbia Indian Residential School Survivors Society, who have advised and supported me in this project.

That said, I would not have undertaken writing *Wawahte* or my first book, *Mile Post 104 and Beyond*, if it were not for a special friend, Gerard (Jerry) Wyatt, a retired professor of biology who shares with me a love of the natural world. He encouraged me to write and then helped to adjust my scribbles into conventional English. Thank you Jerry.

This same appreciation goes to the Baud family, Doug Huddle, Wm. Bruner and Brian Cameron, for their knowledge of books, and constructive critical assessments.

A special Mequietch goes to Jack Ogama for the farewell blessing spoken in Ojibway to our four-year-old son Perry—a Canadian Forces Lieutenant-Colonel. "You will grow to become a soldier-warrior and will fight for the good of people and our land." Perry, your continued help with this project gives honour to an old friend's vision.

Judith Hazlett, a retired lawyer with a background in journalism, and Wayne Jones, for editing and proofreading the revised manuscript—Thank you.

I thank my wife Inge Wells for her encouragement and help during this two-year project. Much love!

Introduction

Esther Speaks

Esther Love (Faries)

Watchea (Hello) ———————— I am Esther. You are reading *Wawahte* today because Bob, an old friend, called me on the telephone and said, "Esther, you are a very special person; you and other Indian residential school survivors have a story that needs to be written." His call was as if the Great Spirit had answered my prayers. I am a very private person. I do not naturally seek recognition or exposure. However, I have worried that soon there would be no one left to tell about how life was for many Aboriginal people living in the boreal forest regions and elsewhere in Canada. I knew that Bob and I would talk and that he would handle my story with honesty and sensitivity.

Wawahte is a non-fiction book. Although this is the story of Bunnie, Stanley and me, it is not unique to the three of us; it was much the same for more than 150,000 Aboriginal children who, between 1883 and 1996, were forced to attend 130 residential schools across Canada.

As a child, my home was Mammamattawa Village, also called English River Village/Indian Reserve. That was until a man came one day and took me, along with other children, to live at Pelican Lake Indian Residential School near Sioux Lookout, Ontario.

As Elders reflecting back on events in our lives, we no longer need to do so in anger. We are eternally grateful that the wrongs of the past have been acknowledged. The Indian Residential Schools Settlement Agreement has blazed a trail for all to make a better future. All three of us in our own way say, "You cannot be wholly angry if you are grateful for the life skills learned, especially now that Aboriginal people and all Canadians have been given the vision to see a morning sunrise that gives the promise of a better day."

We have done everything possible to tell our stories truthfully. *Wawahte* is our legacy and our gift to present and future generations to help both young and old to better understand a piece of Canada's history that will soon be lost from living memory.

Wawahte is written differently than most books. Throughout, there are words in the Cree language like "watchea" which means "hello" Following each Cree language word is the corresponding English word followed by a space. The space is for you to write the word in your ancestral language if it is not Cree or English. If you do not know your ancestral language then ask an Elder.

Native Elders' wisdom says: "To know your language is to know your culture." I challenge you to make the effort to accept this gift. You will be happy you did.

Sighgetan (Love) _____, *Esther*

Prologue

The Author
Robert P. Wells

"I didn't do anything bad. Papa, why do these people not like me?
Papa got a very sad look on his face and looked as if he was trying
not to cry."

The Golden Eagle feather, held sacred by Canada's First People, and two Canadian flags appearing on the book's cover is a statement, that Canada too, has a dark chapter of racial history:

> *Racism takes many arrangements. When it rises from simply being the opinion of a handful of people to becoming widely accepted by a nation, it can and did, result in an official program that was to the public touted as beneficial, but actually discriminated against and tried to extinguish an entire ethnic group—Canada's original residents. (Excerpted in part from: The US Review of Books—Wawahte—reviewed by John E. Roper[1]).*

I try here to answer the question about "the why" and "the how" concerning seven generations of children forced by law to attend residential schools, the present-day challenges of identity, social dysfunction, ownership of the land and resources, First Nation self-determination, and so on.

Growing up in the 1940s and '50s at my family's fishing lodge in northwestern Ontario was very different from what my life is now. We were isolated, living in roadless Quetico, 104 miles down the railroad track from now Thunder Bay. We did not have the convenience of indoor plumbing,

---

[1]   http://www.theusreview.com/reviews/Wawahte-Wells.html.

electricity, or stores. There was more work to everyday living. Neighbours were few and far between. As children, we spent much of the time outdoors entertaining ourselves.

As a child I was not aware of what a special place and friends I had. The trees and water were there to play with or to use for whatever was needed. The colour of my skin being white did not make me different from my Indian friends whose skin was brown. Even if it did, it would only be in some joking way. To think of your backyard as enchanting or special was absurd; it was just there—a part of everyday life. Whatever nature threw at you, you adjusted life to accommodate it. The only times I vividly remember as exciting and looked forward to with anticipation were spring break-up and fall freeze-up[1]. This truly marked the end of one season and the beginning of the next. When I was finally sent out to a school in the big city of Milwaukee, Wisconsin, I remember feeling cheated because I was not in the bush during the fall freeze-up.

As I grew older, I was more and more aware of what special friends I had. How much my friends and growing up in the Canadian bush are a part of who I became. I would never want it to be otherwise. I married Inge, who was born in Germany, and we became parents to a blue-eyed blond-haired boy whose out-of-doors play language was Anisinabek[2]. My Aboriginal friends, my life as a fishing and hunting guide, fur trapper, and twenty-eight years as an Ontario Conservation Officer have resulted in my appreciation for nature and an interest in First Nation(s) culture[3] and their history.

I sometimes think that I am fated to see both sides from the middle. Showing my childhood friend Moochum Joe the early beginnings of my shoebox collection of *The Beaver* magazine clippings about "Indians", Moochum said, "Nabis (boy), you have an unusual curiosity about us. Your spirit is different from all the other white kids we know—we talk about that".

Little did I know that, sixty-five years later, a family genealogy would reveal that I was not all that "white". My great-grandmother Marie (eleven times removed) was a Mi'kmaq. The discovery of my native heritage was welcome, as was the impact of a wise old Elder telling me as a child, "You, Nabis, have been given spiritual guidance to someday draw words on paper—tell your kind how bad Indian people are treated. They take our kids away—they not allow us to live as who we are."

Moochum, your spirit lives—I shall try to light-the-light for all to know. You saw purpose to my treasured *Beaver* clipping collection—Mequietch old friend, Nabis.

I had a difficult time organizing my thoughts about the story of forced integration, Indian residential schools, and the post-generational impacts. I strongly believe that the pervasive problems of alcoholism, drug use, domestic violence, and high rates of incarceration and suicide are not First Nation problems alone. They are a problem for all Canadians. Those of us who are not personally affected need more than a clip on the evening news that something isn't right on some Indian Reserve somewhere back in the bush.

Surely, we have become sufficiently mature not to hide from this dark chapter of colonial history. The time has come to chart a new course. The history of forced integration and residential schools, and the history of Canada's first people ought to be taught in all Canadian schools.

Robert P. Wells

Prologue: Terminology and End Notes:

In Canada, Aboriginals were commonly referred to as "Indians" until the 1980s. The Canadian Constitution (*The Constitution Act, 1982*) *recognizes three groups of Aboriginal peoples—Indians (status and non-status), Métis, and Inuit. "First Nations" is a legally defined term that came into common usage in the 1980s to replace the term "Indian Band".* As individuals, First Nations people are officially recognized by the Government of Canada as "registered Indians" or "status Indians" if they are listed on the *Indian Register* and are entitled to benefits under the *Indian Act.*

"Indian" is still a legal term in the *Indian Act.* However, its use is on the decline in Canada. Some First Nations people consider the term "Indian" offensive. Though an overgeneralization, many First Nation people meeting one another for the first time, will usually ask, "What nation are you from?"—replying "What" and from "Where".

(1) "Break-up" and "Freeze-up" are terms used to describe when a lake or river clears itself of ice in the spring or freezes over in late fall.

(2) "Anisinabek"—*Anishinabe*, Chippewa, Ojibway, Ojibwe, and Ojibwa. What do these words mean? There is no difference. All these different spellings refer to the same

people. In Canada more people use "Ojibway." In the United States more people use "Chippewa," All six of these spellings are common. They all come from the Algonquian language.

(3) "Culture provides people with a sense of belonging, a connection to their Creator and each other, and a feeling that they are part of something bigger than their individual selves." (Reference: Lynda Gray—First Nation 101 (2012)—page 22)

Part One

Esther's Story

I begin my story by telling about the happy day-to-day family life of my childhood growing up on the land. Later I move on to tell about a child's experience of being taken from her family, and what life was like at an Indian Residential School.

My birthplace was the Cree[1] and Oji-Cree Hudson's Bay Post village of Mammamattawa, located on the Kenogami River. Referred to as an Indian Reserve[2], Mammamattawa was 10 kilometers south of the uninhabitable swampy land that had been designated as English River Indian Reserve No. 66. People here lived isolated in the bush 100 kilometers north of the Canadian National Railroad Line, between James Bay and Lake Nipigon in Northern Ontario. The village was accessible only by canoe in the summer and snowshoes or dog team in the winter. Supplies were brought in by river barge during the spring high-water periods. The only thing that makes the village more accessible in the twenty-first century is the airplane, but that doesn't matter as no one lives there anymore. In the 1930s, the place was home to about twenty families, the Faries (my family), Stephens, Solomon, Sutherland, Bluff, Rubin, Goodwin, Puninish, Iserhohh, Taylor, Buff, Westley, and Mattwas.

Most people did not live in our village year round. They lived on their trapping grounds during the winter and in river camps during the summer. This was at a time when very few rural people—white or Aboriginal—had cars, electricity, running water, refrigerators, or other conveniences . . . Snowmobiles, televisions, computers had not yet been invented or were not available. This was a time when airplanes were so uncommon that people ran outside to look up when they heard one flying overhead. Life was not simpler than now, but it was different.

People might think that it would be boring for the kids, as well as adults, not to have computer games, television, books, radios, or even a clock. I have no childhood memory of ever being bored, my family lived as one with nature, and there were always things that had to be done. Almost everything we needed to live we got directly from the land and waters. We did not have the luxury of idle time to become bored. In those days my family and most other native people survived with the use of very little money.

The money we did earn in the winter by fur trapping was used to buy tea, flour, sugar, oatmeal, and some clothing. Papa bought equipment for hunting and trapping from the Hudson's Bay Trading Post in the village.

This was not a romantic life in a natural paradise, as some might like you to believe. I grew up in the severe and unforgiving environment of Northern Ontario—a land cold in winter and insect infested in summer. My people lived by the collective wisdom and skills learned and passed down through many generations: For example: "humility—respect—honesty—wisdom—love—truth—courage."

At the time there was an abundance of fur-bearing animals that were harvested and sold to a very demanding world fur market. Each family unit had traditional areas where they hunted and trapped.

We were hunters, caregivers, gatherers, craftspeople, jokesters, and storytellers. People seemed at place into the roles that best suited them, their family, and the community. The community of Mammamattawa built an Anglican church and Reverend Clark was our minister. When he was off visiting other communities, lay Elders would lead church services. Parents, grandparents, and the community taught the children about nature, about how get along as a family, how to make and do things that nowadays people buy and pay others to do for us. Playtime taught children skills that they would need to know when they became adults. The boys played at hunting, fishing, and wilderness field craft. Girls in turn made play of "women's work"—preparing food, sewing, gathering, and being a good mother. But, nobody played at the daily jobs of gathering wood and water.

The traditional homeland, language, culture, spiritual beliefs, folklore, and family structures were strong. I don't suppose that there was a family more closely united in love and mutual understanding and respect than mine. I remember daily life as being a constant ripple-of-giggles.

I will tell you about the happy and sad time of my childhood in the hope that you will better understand what parents and elders now talk about. What it was really like to live on the land. What it was really like to be taken from your parents, put on a train, and to be carried off to an Indian Residential School. These institutions were places notorious for beating children that spoke their Indian language when they knew no other way to talk. A place where children were made to look into the eyes of people in authority, when their parents and Elders had taught them that to do so was disrespectful. This was a terrible thing to do to parents, and the residential school was, for most, an awful place to be as a child. There is something fundamentally wrong with separating children from their parents. I still ask, "Why?"

———————————

Esther's Story: End Notes

1. The Cree: The largest group of First Nations in Canada with over 200,000 members and Cree 135 First Nations. Originally inhabiting a small nucleus in the Great Lakes region of what is now Canada, the Cree Nation expanded rapidly in the 17th and 18th centuries after acquiring firearms and beginning their fur trade with the Europeans. Later, as their contact with fur traders and the church clergy exposed them to smallpox, influenza, and tuberculosis, to which they had no protective biological immunity, their numbers were reduced. It has been estimated that severe smallpox epidemics in 1784 and 1838 reduced the Cree by more than forty percent.

2. Indian Reserve: Tract of land, the Crown, set apart for the use and benefit of a First Nation. The Crown retains legal title.

Mammamattawa Village

I was born in 1931, the second child of William and Emily Faries of the Faries family of Cree ancestry in the village of Mammamattawa, Ontario. My Status Indian [1] Registration Number is 1,820,067,501. The name Faries, not of Aboriginal heritage, comes from my great-grandfather, a Scotsman. In some ways, not knowing my ancestral name troubles me, but I have come to realize that a name alone doesn't define who or what we are as a person.

My mother died when I was about four or five years old. Throughout my life the sadness of my mother dying never completely left me. There has been and there always will be a hole in my heart. It was a very difficult time for Papa, my brothers Gilbert and Richard, and my sister Greta. The people of the village were all very nice and they came together to help Papa look after us kids and to help make our sadness go away. Sometime later Papa married Alice. She became our mama and I got another sister, Caroline.

Emily, baby Esther and William Faries (1931)

Most homes in the village were either tents or buildings with log walls, canvas tent roofs, and dirt floors. Stanley Stephen, who also grew up in the village, tells that his Moochum (grandfather) _____ lived in a tent his whole life; he ate and slept, in our traditional way, on the ground. Our family home was one of the more permanent built homes in the village, a two-room house made from logs with glass windows, board floors, and a wood and tarpaper roof. Mama, Kukum (grandmother), _____ Papa and Moochum slept in the big room that was about 6m by 8m and the kids slept in the little room.

In the village there was a Hudson's Bay Company Trading Post and an Anglican Church. The only mistickcuoshow (white-people) _____ living here at the time were Reverend Neville Clark, the pastor of the Anglican Church, his wife Alice, their three little girls, and the Hudson's Bay Company Manager[2]. There had been a great effort by the Churches to convert our people to Christianity, a concept quite different from Cree tradition.

The people accepted the one-God and one-devil teachings of the church, but at the same time, most never gave up their ancestral spirituality[3] and beliefs.

Elders built the village's first church as a place to worship and a statement for all to see that we were Christians. This church was so small that not all the people could be inside at the same time. Many had to stand outside to attend services.

Six years before I was born, the people in the village began building the "big" church, so everyone could be inside to attend services. Elders went up the river to cut long logs for the foundation of the church and they cut the short logs for walls from the forest near where the church was built. The walls were built from standing logs that they cut square with an axe. There were no sawmills in the area to make boards so most buildings were made without boards and the use of nails. This was at a time when, each spring during high water, the Hudson's Bay Company would barge the annual supplies for the village down the river. The barges were made from lumber that came by train to the town of Pagwa from British Columbia and were put together with nails. The barges would remain where they were unloaded, because they could not travel against the river's current, since they were not equipped with engines.

The Hudson's Bay Company gave the community Elders permission to use the barges to build their church. The barges were taken apart and the lumber and nails were used to make the roof and floor; it took years to complete the building of the new church. The bishop sold the old church, no longer needed, to hunters.

When I was a little girl, Reverend Clark and his family lived in three small rooms that were attached to the back of church. When Reverend Clark went preaching along the river, Elders David Solomon, Elizabeth Sutherland, Nayes Rubin, and John Wesley-Abbin did the preaching. There were services three times a day, morning, afternoon, and evening, three times a week.

Reverend Clark had a very nice personality and people were glad that he wanted to learn to speak our Cree language. He sent away for books on how to write the Cree language and then taught writing to both children and adults. Cree people, as all Aboriginal people in what is now Canada, did not have a written language before the arrival of Europeans. The written Cree language was created by an early Christian cleric using Syllabic as opposed to the Roman alphabet: For example (◁-a) (▽-e) (△-I).

Getting the people to church on "clock-time" was a challenge for Reverend Clark. Like most people in the village, our family did not own a clock, or know clock and calendar time. The sun was our clock and nature our calendar. In the beginning, people watched for neighbours to straggle off to the church and would in turn follow them. This quite simply meant that few if anyone got to church on Reverend Clark's clock-time. Reverend Clark decided that "Indian-time" was a far too casual way to schedule God's work so he introduced us to the church bell to signal people when it was time to come to church services. On Sunday people were expected to go to services three times. Reverend Clark instructed the congregation that his first bell ringing was a signal to put on coats and the second was to begin walking to the church. The people thought this was funny and made jokes about Reverend Clark's bell-time but they went along to please him.

Most of my childhood memories about church are Christmas, Easter, Mama going to live in heaven, and for me "not to make sins." As children, we believed that if it were not for Reverend Clark and his church, Santa Claus and the Easter Bunny would never have known where to find us. I remember all the kids going to the church to see the beautiful Christmas tree decorated with pretty ornaments,

Santa Claus coming during the night when we were asleep leaving each child candy and a toy that his elves had put into little burlap bags. We stayed up late for midnight church service, the big feast and eating Christmas pudding, the adults step dancing, and me waking up in my own bed not remembering going home. Most of all, I remember Papa telling me about the secret of the Wawahte. I was very young at the time and have no actual memory of that Christmas Eve but I remember well his telling of it. Holding my hand, as our family walked home from Christmas night church service, we stopped. Papa said, "Look up Esther, see the dancing lights in the sky. They are people who have died and are now on their after-life spirit journey. Some of the dancing-lights are our ancestors and they have come tonight to see and dance for you. They are telling you, Esther, that they love you, they wish you Merry Christmas and ask that you always remember to pray that their after-life journey will be to nice places." In troubled times, I have found great comfort in looking to the Wawahte. Thank you, Papa, for only you know my grief when Mama went on her journey into the spirit world. The spirit angels then and many times since have lifted me to my feet when my wings had trouble remembering how to fly. Meeg-wetch.[4] (Thank You)

_____.

The people in our village lived an unregimented lifestyle, with little interference from the outside world. Elders, a name given to the older and the wiser people, were recognized community and family leaders. This is not to say that there was no competition, for there was a competitive pride in all that we did. Though there was great respect given to Elders, there was no authority figure in the village. This is not to say that Reverend Clark did not try to become that person. At this time the village did not have a chief, band council or a government-appointed Indian Agent telling people what and when to do things. The community functioned by a mutual understanding of respect and co-operation, as had been the way for generations.

Everyone in the community watched over the children. Children were seldom disciplined and would never be scolded or beaten; a stern look or word from a parent or community elder would bring silence to the usually wound-up chatter of children. Everyone respected differences. This was not to say that folks did not talk and laugh about one another—in particular about Reverend Clark—because they all did. It was the way it was.

Alcohol was extremely rare in the village. If someone did get drunk and behave like a fool one day, people thought no less of the person the following day when their behaviour was back to normal.

Thousands of years of ancestral tradition had taught the Indigenous[5] people inhabiting the regions of the north how to create their own personal living space in their mind and non-aggressive coping skills. By their nature, most people were able to accept and tolerate others for whom and what they might be. So many people living together, in what we now consider very small houses, might be considered stressful, but then it was seldom seen to be. I remember my parents always to be busy. When Mama and Kukum were not looking after kids or cooking and cleaning, they would hand stitch, with linen thread, moccasins, mittens, hats, vests, and coats. These garments were made from rabbit skins and the amber-coloured, smoked, tanned moose and caribou hides prepared during the summer when we lived by the river. What I remember most are the beautiful glass beads and decorative yarn adornments inspired by our culture that they stitched to our mittens and vests. Our dresses, shirts, and undergarments they made from old dresses, and sugar and flour bags. Sometimes Mama and Kukum would buy sewing material from the Hudson's Bay Trading Post.

I do not know if the Hudson's Bay Trading Post was responsible for establishing our village, or if it were put there because the village was already there. In any event, this was where people bought the things they needed and sold the skins of the animals they trapped. It was mostly the pelts of the beaver and the muskrat that the Hudson's Bay Company was founded upon. Each spring, after the ice was gone from the lakes and rivers, people came by canoe from far away to sell their furs to the Hudson's Bay Trading Post. As did everybody else in the village, we sold our furs to Hudson's Bay. Like the others, we never received much money once the books were squared for the things we bought on credit throughout the year. The next year the cycle would begin all over again. The Hudson's Bay Company had a saying at the time, "Never give an Indian too much credit in case it would be cheaper for him to move than to pay his bill."

This was a very unkind way for them to think about us, as my Papa and Moochum were very proud and honourable people, though they resented owing their soul to the Hudson's Bay Company. It would have never occurred to them not to honour their commitments. If not having much money meant we were poor—then we were poor. But I contend that we were anything else but poor. I had a loving family that cared for and looked after us. We knew how to live respectfully on and from the land and waters, and we did. We did not hunt and fish for recreation or fun; it was our way of life and our means of survival. Moose, caribou, and rabbit were winter fare and their hides provided warm winter garments. Nothing was wasted.

When Mama was expecting my brother Richard, Papa made a frame for his tickanogon (cradle) _____ from the sacred wood of a cedar tree. My mother and grandmother attached beautiful beaded smoke-tanned moose calf leather to the cradle frame. Babies were placed in a tickanogon and carried on the mother's back.

The tickanogon is a great way to carry a baby in the bush as it can be hung in a tree or leaned beside a rock when picking blueberries or washing clothes in the river. We tied dangly things to the protective hoop to entertain the baby. They would swing and jiggle as Mama walked. Papa and Moochum also made the girls little cradles for us to carry our dolls in, and we learned how to be mothers by growing up playing with dolls and watching Kukum and Mama love and care for us.

We did not use baby diapers; moss was gathered from the bush, cleaned of sticks, dried, and used as baby diapers are today. Moss is absorbent and our babies never got diaper rash. We bathed ourselves by using a wash dish and took our baths in winter in a laundry tub and in summer in the river. We kids all took our turn taking our laundry tub bath in the same water that our brothers and sisters had bathed in, think what you like. Even though we lived a primitive life style we kept our bodies clean. My Moochum would sometimes get up and come to the table to eat without first washing his hands. Mamma would say, "Moochum, wash your hands before you eat at our table," he would say, "I have no need to wash," and insist that he hadn't been doing anything with his hands. Mama would say sternly, "Moochum, you are not eating at my table until you wash your hands," and he would sheepishly go to the wash dish and scrub his hands that were twisted and scarred from work, just to please Mama.

As soon as he finished, everybody would laugh. Moochum laughed the loudest.

Papa and Moochum would sit together talking and making things when they were not outside looking after our ten sleigh dogs. Our dogs were very special to Papa and he cared for them well. They ate rabbit, moose, and caribou meat and something like porridge that my parents cooked for them. Unlike most of our neighbours' sleigh dogs, our dogs did not eat fish.

Papa and Moochum would visit neighbours and talk about trapping, hunting, and stuff that men talk about and we would learn from their talk, from watching, and them showing us how to do things. Though children education was informal, as we did not have a school, everyone in our community taught us how to do things, make things, and the lessons to be learned from the land.

Fur trapping was most important, as there was no other way for us to earn money. Though we lived mostly off the land, hunting, fishing, and gathering food, we did require some money to live. The world, at the time, was in the middle of the Great Depression and there was no welfare, as we know it today. Treaty Indians, meaning that, as individuals we were registered as being Indian, were entitled to receive $4.00 per year Treaty Money from the federal Department of Indian Affairs. More often than not it would cost more than $4.00 for people like us living in the bush to go and get it. The depression and the World War II years (1939-1945) were an impoverished time of sacrifice and doing without. There was little or no work during the Depression years anywhere in Canada, let alone on a remote reserve. This was also a time long before our people earned money—guiding tourists coming north to fish and hunt. My parents, as others in our village, earned enough money each winter trapping to buy very basic food items, tools and equipment such as cooking pots, snare-wire, bullets, and blankets.

People have often asked me, what did you eat back in the old days when there was no pizza, hot dogs, or ready-to-eat food such as we now buy in stores? When we were living in the village or out in the bush trapping, my mother and grandmother made rabbit, beaver, moose, or caribou stew with dumplings they thickened with rolled oats. Sometimes onions, carrots, and potatoes were added. They also made bannock[6] every day. That was especially good with raisins. We drank tea but didn't always have sugar. I have no memory of ever being hungry when I was with my parents as we always had plenty to eat. We did not have fresh or canned milk, so mothers nursed their babies until they were old enough to eat regular food. Our mothers would give us fish juice to drink, made by boiling sturgeon in salted water and straining off the liquid. As awful as drinking fish juice may seem to you, it was nutritious and something we learned to like.

I remember that Moochum had the only garden in the village, our only off-limit place to play. Agriculture was not a part of Cree culture and was something that Moochum had learned from white folks. Late each summer, with people watching, Moochum proudly harvested our yearly supply of potatoes from his little garden.

———————————

Mammamattawa Village: End Notes

1. Status Indians are people who are entitled to have their names included on the Indian Register, an official list maintained by the federal government. Certain criteria determine who can be registered as a Status Indian. Only Status Indians are recognized as Indians under the Indian Act, which defines an Indian as "a person" pursuant to the Act.

2. Hudson's Bay Company Trading Post Managers were called "Factors."

3. "The key difference between First Nations worshiping practices and non-First Nation practice(s) is the formality of how it was promoted and expressed. Traditional First Nation practice is more accurately described as spirituality rather than religion as the main emphasis is on the spiritual connections with the Creator. It is not based on hierarchies, blame, shame, or male dominance. Rather, it is based on building and maintaining the spiritual self and fulfilling responsibilities as beings on this earth by being connected to and caring for the land, each other, ancestors, other living beings such as animals, plants, and the Creator in daily life." (Reference: Lynda Gray—First Nation 101 (2012)—page 26.)

4. "Meeg-wetch" meaning "thank you" in English has a variety of spellings: "Meeg-wetch" is a usual Cree/English spelling whereas "Miigiwetch" and Mequietch are spellings that are often used by the Anishinabek and others.

5. Indigenous here means "People native to the area." And, Non-Aboriginal: Anyone who is not an Aboriginal person.

6. Bannock: a type of bread made without yeast, with flour and water and cooked in a frying pan or on a stick over an open fire.

Fur Trapping and the Summer by the River

All the trappers agreed not to trap and hunt in each other's traditional trapping areas. People not only respected traditional family trapping and hunting areas but helped one another to be successful if bad luck fell upon someone.

Each fall and early winter, Papa and Moochum would go alone to our trapping areas to catch beaver, mink, martin, and foxes and to shoot moose and caribou. The family stayed behind in the village. The men would come home for a while in early winter and wait until winter really set in and then we would all go to live in the bush on our trapping area. It was exciting for us kids to travel by dog sled and to go live at Papa's bush camp. It did not matter that it was very cold. Our dog team would be harnessed up, and we would be on our way. The baby was in his cradle and my brothers and I were wrapped in rabbit skin blankets. Even the dogs showed their excitement. The pups, born in the spring and too young to be harnessed to pull the sled, ran untied, alongside the team.

While on the trapping grounds we lived in a big tent that Papa and Moochum had set up when they went fall and early winter trapping. The place they would select for our winter camp was sheltered from the wind, near both water and dry standing firewood. Winter camps were set up in thick stands of short evergreen trees, with the tent opening facing the south. Care was taken when selecting a site for winter camp, to avoid large trees, which might fall on our tent or the dogs, tied nearby.

The tent was kept warm by a wood-burning stove called an airtight heater that we also used to cook on. We slept on the ground on beds made from the branches of spruce trees and we covered ourselves with blankets made from rabbit skins. Everyone had a pair of snowshoes that Papa and Moochum made during the summer. It was a must to remember to always to put the snowshoes up high, out of reach of the dogs, as they would destroy them by eating the rawhide webbing that was made from non-smoked tanned moose and caribou skins. We took similar precautions with our beaver pelts that we laced onto hoops and put outside to frost dry. The dogs were always kept tied, but occasionally one would get loose.

Life at our bush camp was different than in the village. We played less, spending more time outside doing real jobs. There were dogs to feed, water to carry, wood to cut, rabbit snares to check, and partridges to hunt. For my people to survive the very cold winter nights that I now know would dip the thermometer to -40 degrees Celsius and colder, it was our custom to cut our firewood daily, unless, Moochum said, "there was a storm coming", and we then would cut enough wood to last three days.

I have heard two non-Aboriginal explanations for us "Indians" not cutting and piling our winter firewood like white people. First, "Indian" people are lazy people. I know this not to be true. You could not be lazy and still survive winters in northern Canada. Their other explanation is that if we cut and piled wood outside then others would come and take it. This act is not considered stealing in many traditional Aboriginal communities in the north. There may be some truth to the second one, but I believe that the reason for cutting wood daily came from a long forgotten wisdom to survive the winter doldrums. This daily activity got the people outside of our traditionally small, overcrowded winter quarters when there would be little reason to go outside. My people were and are a tough and enduring people. We knew how to survive the harsh and unforgiving climate of northern Canada. My ancestors had done so for hundreds of years—not by being lazy.

The men spent most days out setting and checking their traps. The women and kids would stay near camp. Mama would take the older kids with her to snare rabbits, to shoot squirrels and partridge, and to cut wood while Kukum would stay with the baby in the tent. As you can appreciate, it took a lot of food to feed all of our sled dogs and us. So Papa and Moochum would always try to ensure we had enough moose and caribou meat, but sometimes when we did not have enough meat, we would have to eat beaver meat.

Winter in Northern Ontario is long and cold, and the days are short—something that my people seemed to accept without complaint and the same can be said about the mosquitos the north is so infamous for. It was the way it was, part of nature and not something to complain about. It may just be one of the universal truths accepted by people, living one with nature, accepting what you cannot change. This was something I found to be quite different when I became exposed to white people. After saying hello, white people would complain about the weather. I must admit, I now also complain about such things.

This was a wonderful time in my life. My family was close and we did things together. We learned from our parents and the community how to live in harmony with one-another and with nature. The Creator created the waters, forests and the creatures for all to use and to respect. We took our food and water from the forest and lakes without worries about pollution.

Late in the winter, before spring break-up, we would all move back to the village and wait for the arrival of spring and summer. Each spring some of our sleigh dogs would have puppies. They were very special and we loved to play with them.

The closer we got to summer the more excited the people became about going camping on the river. Every summer, my family lived in tents on the shoreline of the Pagwa River[1]. Living beside lakes and rivers during the summer and moving to more sheltered locations back in the bush for the winter was the long practiced lifestyle of my ancestors because access to food, fur trapping, and shelter from the cold north wind were a necessity. We moved from our winter campsite to live alongside lakes and rivers in the summer, where we would catch fish, hunt animals that came to drink and feed, and ensure there was a breeze that gave us some relief from the pesky mosquitos. In the winter, we spent some time outside each day, but in the summer, except for sleeping, we were seldom inside during the day. The warm weather of spring always reminds me of how good it felt to shed my many layers of heavy winter clothing and go outside without first having to dress.

You may wonder now about children and their usual excitement about things to come when we did not have a calendar to count off the days. It was not only the children but also grownups that became excited about things to come, especially going to live on the river. Getting anxious, upset, or excited was most unusual, as the Cree people lived a relaxed life-style. The only exception I can remember of adults showing outward signs of being excited was about getting ourselves prepared to go live on the river. Moochum and Kukum would ask each other, did you pack this or that. Moochum would go ten times a day to check that our canoes were okay. Papa only went to check on the canoes two or three times a day. There was excitement everywhere in the village. We kids knew that we would soon be leaving for summer camp. Reverend Clark came to tell us that God was watching over us, to remember to say our prayers and to live with Jesus in our hearts.

On moving day the adults loaded our summer supplies and equipment in cedar-plank-and-canvas-covered rib canoes. The kids were responsible for rounding up all the puppies and our own canoe paddles. The puppies rode in our canoe and the big dogs ran along the river shoreline. One might assume that the puppies' mothers would become defensive when we separated them from their pups but they seemed to know what was happening. It may have been that they trusted us kids as we had played with their puppies from the time they were born.

It took us two days to reach the summer campsite, making it necessary to camp one night on the way there and even longer if it rained. Stopping in early afternoon, Papa would first set his gill net in the river to catch fish for our evening meal. Although we always carried food with us, we fished, hunted, or gathered food each day to eat. We set up our first night's camp on the same side of the river that the dogs ran along so that they would not have to swim across the river to reach their puppies. Papa wanted our whole family to ride in his canoe; Mama paddled in the bow of the canoe, Papa in the stern, and we kids along each side. Papa had made the kids little canoe paddles and everyone except the baby helped paddle the canoe. We must have looked real funny going down the river with so many paddles dipping in and out of the water on each side of the canoe.

Moochum and Kukum paddled their own canoe. We usually arrived at summer camp late in the afternoon of the second day. This was such a beautiful place for the five or more families to spend the summer, with a sand beach for the kids to play on and river rapids to sing us to sleep at night.

Whoever was first from the village to arrive at river camp, after unloading their canoes, would set gill nets below the rapids to catch fish for everybody's evening meal. On our arrival, Mama and Kukum would set up our tents with the help of others who may have arrived before we did. We kids first saw that the puppies got back with their mothers, went looking for animal tracks along the riverbank, and treasures we had hidden in the bush the summer before.

The people from our village camped at one of two sites on the river that were about eight kilometers apart. We visited back and forth and shared with one another. Papa, as did other men, would shoot a small moose or caribou that would be shared with people from both camps. We did not have any means of refrigeration and meat had to be eaten or smoke-cured to prevent it from spoiling. The hides of animals were put in the river to make the hair easier to remove. Once the hair was scraped off, Mama and Kukum smoke-tanned the skins, making them into soft leather that was made into clothing during the winter.

Our way was simple, and except in the summer, we began each day at dawn. Adults went to bed about one hour after dusk for their first sleep, followed by about a two-hour waking period. They would get up, talk, sometimes made tea, and then retire for a second sleep, waking at sunrise. We kids were encouraged to sleep the whole night through. In the summer when the days were long and the nights short, people mostly slept when they were tired.

We ate when we became hungry and we did not eat when we were not hungry. Breakfast was usually porridge with canned Carnation milk. If we did not have milk, which was most of the time, Mama made the porridge real thin and we ate it without milk. Our late-day meal, called supper, was usually bannock and fish or meat. Mama made stew from the meat of moose, caribou, ducks, partridge, rabbit or fish. We drank tea that I liked best with sugar. If we did not have vegetables to put in the stew, Mama thickened it with porridge or flour that always seemed plentiful. When we became hungry during the day, we snacked on bannock, meat, berries, and, yes, sometimes in the summers that yummy fish juice. During blueberry time, Mama made really good blueberry pancakes. We drank water straight from the rivers and lakes, as the waters had not yet become polluted by industrialization.

We killed animals, birds, and fish to eat, as my people had always done. We did so thankfully, for if we did not, we would not eat. We did not think of ourselves as the boss over nature. I don't ever remember hearing anyone say they were sorry to have killed a moose or caribou, but I do remember my Papa respectfully saying thank you to a little moose that he had just shot, for giving its life, so his family could eat—solemn moment.

This was a great place to spend the summer. The kids had other kids to play with and the adults did what adults do during the day—fishing, hunting, gathering firewood for cooking, tanning hides, fixing meals, and visiting with one another. In the evenings people would come together around a campfire telling stories, and laughing. There was always lots of laughing. Moochum would read from his Bible that was written in the Cree language and sing hymns. He was quite religious, as were most of the people from the village.

We no longer performed traditional drumming and drum dancing. Despite popular opinion, not all First Nation cultures are the same, neither are their ways of expressing culture through songs, dance, spirituality or religion.

We bathed and played in the river but did not go swimming, as very few people knew how to swim even though we canoed most everywhere we went. I don't remember ever hearing of someone accidently tipping over in their canoe. The only thing wrong with summer was that it ended too soon.

One summer's day when I was six years old we put all our stuff in canoes and left English River Village never to return. Papa had built us a two-story house in the town of Pagwa and we were going to live there. It took several days of hard paddling against the current of the Pagwa River [1] to reach our new home.

Pagwa had a train station, and more people than English River Village. There were two churches; lots of wemistikoskiw (white-people) and many of the Aboriginal people spoke English. The community was divided—Aboriginal and white—Anglican and Roman Catholic. I never understood why I was allowed to play with white kids but not with those that went to the Roman Catholic Church. I played with them anyway.

By then Mama had died and Papa had married Alice who had three children. Our new house had one big room downstairs where we cooked, ate, and sat around talking and making things. There were two bedrooms downstairs, one where Papa slept with our new Mama and the other where Moochum and Kukum slept. All of the kids slept on mattresses and blankets on the floor in the one big room upstairs.

I remember Pagwa as a fun place to live. There were lots of kids to play with, the river was close enough for us to go canoeing, and there were trains that came and went. As I was older now, Papa began talking to me about going to school and getting an education so that I could get a good job when I grew up. He also encouraged me to learn to speak English. Often when Papa and Moochum were talking together and I came near them they would switch from talking Cree to speaking English. Learning to speak English was difficult because most of my friends spoke only the Cree language.

Shortly after moving to Pagwa, we took a trip to the town of Hearst on the "Local", a mostly unscheduled, whistle-blowing train, with smoke puffing from the chimney. I remember one of the elders calling it the "iron toboggan." The Local had about ten railroad boxcars and a combination passenger coach and baggage car. This was at a time when there were no roads in this area, and the Local was our lifeline to the outside world. The Local would stop to drop off or pick up people and supplies anywhere along the railway line. A wave of a flag, rag, or arm by trappers, prospectors, fishermen, hunters or berry pickers would bring the train to a stop.

People said that the Local was a slow train but I remember how excited we kids got when the train reached the breathtaking speed of 50 kilometers per hour on my first ride. We were going to stay in Hearst for one week to visit friends and relatives and to just look at things. When we arrived, Papa took us to a place in the bush where we set up small tents for sleeping and getting inside when it rained.

Hearst was a much bigger place than Pagwa. In Hearst there were cars and trucks that I had not seen before, several stores and a place called a restaurant where you could go and pay money to eat. It was here that I ate ice cream for the very first time. Not all the people seemed to know each other as many would walk past not even saying hello.

It was during a trip to Hearst that I got the sense I was different and there were some people who did not like me. Later, I asked Papa, "Why do wemistikoskiw look angry when they look at me? Why don't some say thank you when you give them money in the store for something you buy? Why don't they like us? I didn't do anything bad. Papa, why do these people not like me?" Papa got a very sad look on his face and looked as if he was trying not to cry. He said nothing but picked me up and hugged me and said, "I love you Esther." This long-ago realization that I was considered different, and the pain in my father's face, have haunted me—my whole life. I am thankful there was a time in my life when being "Indian" was not something to be ashamed of. Later, I came to know that look as "an Indian straight out of the bush." Little did I know at the time what this was all about, and I still ask—Why?

Fur Trapping and the summer by the River: End Note:

1. Pagwa River: The Pagwa River becomes part of a northward flowing river system that flows into the Albany River and empties into James Bay at Fort Albany. In a straight line, Fort Albany is more than 300 kilometers from English River Village. This was a water highway long before the Europeans came to the region in search of furs and to Christianize the Cree people.

Robert P. Wells

Shattered Innocence . . .

Pelican Lake Indian Residential School

Sioux Lookout, Ontario

That dreadful much-talked-about day in September finally came when my two brothers and I were taken from our home to attend a residential school. I was seven years old. My parents had tried to prepare us for this by telling us that we would be going off to school so that we would get good jobs as adults. Knowing what I know now, I wish that I had hidden so that they could not have found me.

A white-man went from home to home telling parents that he had come to take their children. That afternoon 25 five-to-twelve-year-old children were taken from their parents. We were taken to the Pagwa train station, each with a little burlap bag for a suitcase. There we waited for the train to take us to Pelican Lake Indian Residential School in Sioux Lookout, Ontario—800 kilometers away.

The Local came and we hugged our parents and grandparents goodbye. Papa picked me up in his arms and whispered in my ear that there was no shame in crying, not to do things that would bring me shame, and to keep my spirit proud. This was Papa's special way of telling me to be a good girl and stand proud. Papa had never been to school, but he knew that we were in for a very difficult time.

Our new Mama, Alice, told us to look after each other and to be good. Moochum and Kukum looked down at the ground and did not talk. When we were getting on the train, Papa and Moochum pretended to be happy and laughed to make us feel happy, but I was not happy. I have never forgotten looking out of the train window and seeing my parents crying. There they stood, left behind and helpless to do anything, as they watched the train leave the station with their children. Years later, Papa told me that for a long time after our departure, my Kukum's anguished heart was burdened with the uncertainty of ever seeing us again. This was a very difficult time for everyone and especially for my grandparents. Our people did not understand why their children had to be taken far from them to attend school when some native children were allowed to attend day school with white children in the village.

The men who came and took us did not talk to us. They just pointed and said words that I did not understand. They made the older children who had already attended Residential School sit together and they were not allowed to talk to the children going to the Residential School for the first time. No one was allowed to use the bathroom until the train was a long way from Pagwa. One man stood by the door to keep the older kids from jumping off the train.

I was so scared that I could not stop shaking. The older girls were not allowed to go and comfort the little children who were crying. It was so very sad. Although this happened many years ago, I remember that awful day as if it were yesterday. How could those men be so unkind?

When we arrived in the town of Nakina, we changed trains to a passenger train called the Continental. We did not ride in fancy passenger coaches with the white people but travelled third class in old wooden sleeping coaches. (The only other time I saw these old coaches being used was years later to transport German prisoners during World War II.) When night came, the seats in the coach were folded out and made into beds. The boys slept on one side of the train and the girls on the other. I did not sleep well that night. I cried, as did other children, with my blanket pulled over my head.

My brother Gilbert sat with other boys his age. Like the others he did not talk; his scared and homesick face looked straight ahead as if he were asleep with his eyes wide open. The five-and six-year olds were mostly curled up on their train seats sobbing. It was most unusual for children to ride the train and not be looking out of the windows.

Throughout the night, the Continental passenger train made more stops and more children came into our coach. As we travelled westward, many of the children getting on our train spoke the Anishinabek language and I could not understand them. It sounded like our language but the words were different. These kids were scared too. It was an awful train ride.

It was just before daybreak when we arrived at Pelican Lake Indian Residential School. We walked from where the train let us off to the main school building in the dark. I remember how scared the children became seeing cows for the first time. We were taken to a big room called the sewing room and given a blanket and told to sleep on the floor. After a short nap, they served us a breakfast of porridge and molasses, and then sent us outside to play. It was now daylight and we saw the big school for the first time. I had never before seen a building that big—it was scary.

Anglican Minister Reverend Marshall greeted us at the school. He came to where we were playing outside, shouted at us to line up, and told us to open our mouths so he could see our teeth. When we all began to cry, he turned and walked away.

From here we were taken for cleanup. Like all new arrivals, we were made to completely undress to take a bath and wash our hair in a big bathtub. I was so embarrassed having to be naked and to take a bath with strangers watching me. All the little girls were crying as they stood in line without clothes on. After we finished bathing to the satisfaction of the matron, we were given clean clothes, and they gave us real funny haircuts. The girls' hair was bobbed to above the shoulders making our faces look round and the boys hair was cut very close to their heads, which made their ears stick out.

I think that they burned the clothes that I arrived in as I never saw them again. The clothes they gave me to wear were old, had patches on them, and did not fit me well. One day they took all of us and put coal oil in our hair to kill the head-lice that we might have. We had to keep this stinking coal oil, which burnt our skin, in our hair for several days before being allowed to wash it out.

Even as a seven-year-old girl, I found the way we were treated demeaning. We were being treated as if we were captive wild people that had to be tamed. The clothes my parents dressed me in to come here were almost new and clean, my body was clean, and I did not have lice. In today's terms, I felt like I was being bullied and condemned as a worthless person. I had done nothing, but still they made me feel as if I, in some way, had shamed myself.

My second day at Pelican Lake I was awakened early in the morning by a strange female voice yelling loudly, "Come on, girls, wakey, wakey! Rise and shine." For a brief moment I did not know where I was, but upon opening my eyes to a dormitory full of girls scrambling to get out of single cot beds, I realized I was at the Anglican Pelican Lake Indian Residential School. The woman continued to **shout loudly** at us to be quiet. People were rushing around, getting dressed, going to and coming from the lavatory, when a girl grabbed my arm and pulled me into the line that was being marched off to the dining hall for breakfast.

The same woman who had awakened us came over and shook me and said something in a language that I did not understand. When I told her in Cree that I did not understand her words, she slapped my face and yelled at me. When I again attempted to tell her in Cree that I did not understand, she slapped me again. I was so scared that I did not cry and marched, like the other girls, to the dining hall where we had oatmeal porridge with molasses—but no milk. I wasn't very hungry! That morning, I learned my first lesson on how to survive this place . . . never say anything when being punished or when told what you did was wrong. Keep quiet! If you must cry, hold back your tears until you are alone or with a friend you trust.

In the dining hall, I saw my two brothers sitting separately. I had already accepted this hostile place and knew better than to try to go talk to them. My little brother Richard looked as if he had been crying all night.

From the dining hall we were marched in line back to our dormitory to "make neat and tidy." One of the older girls came and helped me make my bed. As I had never slept in a real bed before, I had no idea what it was to make one. Our few personal items had to be laid out on the bed according to regulation.

Then we were again formed into two lines and marched off—one line went to the classroom and the other to work. If you went to school in the morning you switched places with the work crew in the afternoon.

Somewhere along my march, I was pulled out of line and taken into a school classroom where girls and boys were sitting at desks. Here a cheerful young teacher, Miss Goodwin, asked me for my name and wrote it in a book. I say that Miss Goodwin was cheerful as she was the first person in this horrible place that did not shout or hit me. Being struck by an adult was something that had never before happened to me. The Cree culture is less direct and for an adult to strike a child is unthinkable.

In the afternoon I was taken to the kitchen where I worked alongside other girls peeling potatoes, carrots, and onions. I was also shown how to wash dishes. As I grew older, I did other work in the kitchen, dining hall, and other places. I liked working in the kitchen and decided quite early on that when I grew up I wanted to be a cook.

We went to school two hours a day, Monday through Friday. In my seven years at Pelican Lake Indian Residential School the only academic subjects taught were, English, arithmetic, and religion. The emphasis was on vocational skills and religion. The boys were taught farming and forestry work skills. The girls learned sewing, cooking, and laundry work. And, things we would need to know to work as a domestic house servant. But the first lesson learned was to fear the authority of the people in charge. I quickly learned to march everywhere I went and to talk the way they talked.

I had two choices: run away or accept the inevitable. Understandably, as I was only seven years old, fitting in was my only real option. My first day there, I heard that very bad things happen to kids who were caught running away.

You can see from the residential school picture that it was a three-story building. On the first floor there was a large dining hall and kitchen, a playroom, classrooms, a nursing station with two sick rooms, church chapel, offices, staff and guest quarters. The top two floors were dormitories, with rows of cots. One side of the building was for the boys and the other for girls. The older boys and girls slept in the two large dormitories on the third floor. The younger boys and girls, according to their ages, slept in one of the two small dormitories on the second floor.

Bedtime for the younger children was 7:00 pm, and older children were to be in bed by 8:00 pm. When we all were accounted for, there would be up to sixty of us locked inside a dormitory for the night. The electric generator would be shut off and the few dim light bulbs would die, leaving us in total darkness until daylight. There was one toilet in each dormitory and no sink for washing. If we needed a drink of water during the night we would dip a cup of water from the toilet tank reservoir on the back of the toilet. This was a busy spot. There were times, when you went to get a drink of water, you had to ask the person sitting on it to please lean forward so you could lift the toilet tank lid to dip yourself a cup of water. Times got really bad after we were all made to line up and take a tablespoon of castor oil. The laxative was given whether you needed it or not. Quite naturally, we all had to go to the toilet at about the same time and a squirmy line-dance of kids would form, all waiting their turn at the one and only toilet. There must have been Great Spirit Intervention, because in all my years there, no one in my dormitory ever had an accident.

Each day began as the one before. The matron lady would unlock the door to our dormitory and come in yelling loudly, "Come on girls, wakey-wakey-wakey, rise and shine." Followed by a wild scramble, "Quiet, quiet, no talking," of girls getting dressed, taking turns at going to the toilet and then quickly but quietly lining up like soldiers to be inspected and counted. We would again be lined up, inspected, and counted before going to bed.

Upon hearing the signal that all were accounted for, we would march off to the dining hall for our breakfast of yucky oatmeal porridge and molasses. We were not allowed to talk at mealtime and we had to "eat properly." We were shown how to eat properly by the head dining room matron who would hold up eating utensils and **shout**, "This is a spoon, this is a knife, and this is a fork. When eating, you hold your fork and spoon in your right hand and never, never in your left hand. This is how you take your food from your plate. This is how you put your food in your mouth. Do not ever let me hear you slurp your food—slurp—slurp. If I hear you slurping your food, or ever see you holding your spoon or fork improperly, you will be made to stand in the corner. If I think that you are doing this to be smart you will be made to leave the dining hall without eating. If I catch you a second time, you will stand in the corner on one foot. If you sass, you will leave the dining hall and not be allowed to have your next meal." Even though I understood very little English I knew this was serious.

At every meal there was one of two matrons patrolling back and forth watching for someone to pick up their spoon or fork in their left hand or, God forbid, slurp. If we were served something we did not like, or that made us sick, we were made to sit at the table until we ate it. If we threw up we were made to clean up our mess. Throughout these forced feedings we would repeatedly be hit on the hand with a ruler. Thankfully, some exceptions were made for the five-and-six-year-old children.

It wasn't so much that the food was all that bad, but it was for many, the first time we had eaten white man's food, and we did not like it. In my home, as in many northern Aboriginal communities of that the time, we ate a more traditional diet. We did not keep cattle and did not know dairy products, and preferred meat drippings on bannock rather than butter on bread. Tea and fish juice were more familiar than skim milk. Children liked a mixture of lard and peanut butter to put on their bread. I did not like butter. Bannock was not served. There was a lot of tapioca pudding served. We called it called frogeyes.

Though we raised cattle at Pelican Lake we were seldom served milk and when we were it was only skim milk. As with most of the vegetables that we grew, the cream and whole milk was sold to white people by Reverend Marshall.

It would have been nice to say that my classroom experiences were enjoyable, as I really wanted to learn, but they were not. Actually, the classroom was nothing less than horrible. The teachers, except for Miss Goodwin, were forever screaming. The boys took delight in laughing at any girl who was made to go and stand in the corner, got the strap, had her hair pulled, or, God forbid, cried. As bad as the physical abuse was, it was the shame I felt that hurt me the most.

When I first arrived at this awful place, I did not understand how to measure time using a calendar and clock. I quickly learned that everything here was done "quick and quiet—quiet—quiet" and to a schedule according to the white man's clock and the calendar. It wasn't long before I, like every other kid here, was counting off the days to Saturday, Christmas, and most of all, when we would be going home. The following is our Monday through Friday hourly schedule:

0700 – Morning Wake-up

0730 – Breakfast

0800 – Clean Dormitory and Make Beds

0900 – Classroom or Work Detail

15-Minute Recess

Noon – Lunch

1300 – Classroom or Work Detail

15-Minute Recess

1500 – Playtime

1600 – Supper

1700 – Chapel (Wednesday & Friday)

1830 – Play Room

1900 – Young Children's Bed Time

2000 – Older Children's Bed Time

Personal hygiene was a toothbrush, no toothpaste, Lifebuoy soap, and a once-a-week tub bath. I don't know which was worse, taking a tub bath in cold water or being made to brush our teeth with Lifebuoy soap. There was always a registered nurse at the school who was in charge of the infirmary where we stayed if we became very sick. We were told that in the infirmary they could give us better care and that being in isolation would reduce the risk of people passing their sickness on to the other children and staff. The nurse was in charge of our personal hygiene, and it was she who inspected our dormitories, classrooms, dining hall, and kitchen for cleanliness. The nurse, as well as other staff, talked to us about the importance of cleanliness to reduce sickness, which did not always work. It didn't seem to matter how hard we scrubbed ourselves and cleaned the place: if one person came down with a cold, we all caught colds.

In the seven years that I attended Pelican Lake Indian Residential School I was never aware of an Indian Affairs inspector or a medical doctor ever being on site. A dentist would come occasionally to pull children's teeth. Most of the children were under the age of fourteen and came from rural communities without professional medical services. Children arriving with existing medical conditions or having the need of a doctor would be seen by the nurse—over the years many children died. The children's living, schooling, and working conditions were poorly regulated, which left children vulnerable to abuse.

We enjoyed limited recreation, sports, and crafts. The boys played ice hockey on an outdoor rink. They did not compete with other schools, have hockey uniforms or have warm enough clothing to remain outside for long in the winter. Both the boys and girls played soccer and baseball. We did not have a radio but we did have an old wind-up phonograph in our dorm that, with special permission from the matron, we were allowed to play. At Christmas we all became involved in making costumes, trying out for and putting on a Christmas play, and the special choir. Christmas at the school was one of the few fun times that I remember. We were allowed to talk at the Christmas dinner, which was also attended by the staff. The tables were set with a tablecloth, and we were served a meal of roast beef, mashed potatoes, turnips, and dessert that was Christmas pudding and cake. Each child, awaking Christmas morning, found a stocking with gifts at the foot of their bed. We were allowed to talk "Indian" to one another and the staff spoke kindly to us. Over the years, I have asked myself why it was only at Christmas that we were shown kindness and respect, and not all year long.

Papa always came to be with us at Christmas. He also came to visit two or three other times each school year, which was very expensive for him to do. Except when Papa was at the school, my brothers and I were kept separated from each other. He would stay at the school in one of the rooms kept especially for visitors. It was so nice to be together as a family. Some parents never came to visit their children, and then there were children who never went home summers.

The kids got excited when Papa came. Everyone in the school would gather around to listen to him make beautiful music with his violin. Some of the children knew the words to his songs and would sing along as he played. On one visit the boys asked Papa, would he play his violin and call a round (square) dance, if Reverend Marshall gave his permission. We held a dance. It was so much fun, the boys and girls with their happy faces on, dancing and having fun together. I saw Reverend Marshall smiling for the first and only time as he watched us. Other than Papa's violin no other musical instrument was ever heard at school, except for the church organ. If it were not for Papa's visits and the northern lights of the Wawahte, I would not have been able to survive this place.

Saturdays were play days. Sundays were compulsory religious study days. The girls wore black skirts and white blouses. The boys wore grey pants and white shirts. Sunday was devoted to religious worship, play was not allowed. We also went to Chapel two evenings a week, where we received more religious instruction and sang hymns. My favorite song was *Jesus Loves Me* and I liked singing and listening to Christmas carols.

Reverend Marshall always led Sunday Church services that were quite unlike our Anglican Church in English River Village and Pagwa. Pelican Lake Indian Residential School Church was my most terrifying childhood experience. The first Sunday that we were marched into church, Reverend Marshall was there to greet us with his usual stern look, wearing a black robe and a white man's shirt backwards, and pumping a mechanical screwdriver. He began church service by saying, "I will personally use this to ream out the nose of the first brown-skinned kid caught picking their nose. There will be no nose picking in my church, in front of God and our saviour Jesus Christ." I don't remember much, if anything, of what came later that day in church. Reverend Marshall's religious teachings had nothing to do with the love of God, Jesus, and mankind. It was all about "What will happen to Heathen Indians when they die if they do not listen to me." Reverend Marshall did his scary mechanical screwdriver sermon at the beginning of each school year and several times throughout the year, in case we forgot.

I have disliked Reverend Marshall my whole life for his relentless abuse and the scorn with which he, coldheartedly, undermined my sense of self-worth. This conscience-impaired man of authority assumed that I had bad parents and that "Indians" were uncivilized wild heathens. He systemically ran the school in a way that made children believe that being born "Indian" was a crime. We were victimized and there is no doubt in my mind that this kind of mistreatment is responsible for a lot of today's social damage. My parents were strong believers and practiced Christianity with love and kindness. They taught us to respect all Creation and people, including those who worshipped differently than we did. (Some Aboriginal people when I was a child refused to become Christians.) Though not said in these words, it was a cardinal principle in my family not to think oneself better or worse than people who came from another place, and who looked and spoke differently. I think to this day that Papa possessed the wisdom to believe this to be true, even though we ourselves were discriminated against by white society. He would say, "All people see through the same black-coloured part of the eye and someday the clouds of evil will be taken away and we will all be seen as the same but different."

Runaways

When someone was found to be absent, the place went into lock-down until the child was found and strapped for hiding and for not following the rules. If the missing child was not found, he or she would be considered a runaway and the police would be notified. Reverend Marshall would go on a rampage; anyone thought to be a friend of the runaway would undergo endless questioning about what they knew of the runaway's plan. If Reverend Marshal thought you were withholding information, or worse, not telling the truth, you would soon wish you had been the one who had run-away.

It was mostly boys who ran away and they would usually do so in the fall of the year. Many would escape at night by sliding down from the third floor dormitories on bed sheets tied together. Most runaways were caught and brought back to the school by the police or school staff. Some made it back to their homes, only to be brought back to the school by their parents as they were obligated to do. Some parents hid their children from the authorities. Unfortunately, many died from accidents and exposure, and their parents never learned of their fate.

If a runaway was caught and brought back to the school, what followed was horrible. If the runaway was a boy, we were all brought to the dining hall for a "bench-party." Here we would watch the principal administer punishment. The terrified boy would be made to expose his bare buttocks in front of fellow students and staff and be strapped repeatedly with a meter long heavy leather belt. A total head shaving often followed. The girl runaways who were caught and brought back to the school underwent the same punishment, but in the girls' dormitory. Whatever the punishment, it was intended to establish authority over a ragtag and defeated bunch of kids. This was so obvious by the smug way Reverend Marshal would announce the surrender of those spirit-broken, humiliated boys or girls whom he took such pleasure in beating.

Going Home

Winter and spring, after what seemed to be never ending, we were on the train headed for home. It was wonderful to be with my family and not to be scared, sad and lonely, but life was not the same. Ten months at the residential school had changed us and not for the better.

Before we left for school, my brothers and I spoke our language fluently. When we came back that first summer, my parents and grandparents would talk to us in Cree, and we would answer back in English. We talked back to our parents, argued and hit one another, and did things that we never did before. My parents and grandparents were kind and tried to bring us back to the way we were. They knew we had been through a lot. In their quiet unassuming way, they made us feel whole again. My feeling of shame eventually went away but not the hurt.

During our summer school break, our grandparents would take us to live on the river. They did not ask us to tell what happened at the residential school, nor did we tell them. It was not our custom to complain. Evenings we would sit on the riverbank and watch the water and stars, and Moochum and Kukum would talk and sing to make the bad memories of school go away. In a very traditional way, Moochum would take us back to early childhood by telling stories of the past in the terms of the present. It is for this reason that I now recall vivid details of my earliest childhood. I give thanks to the wisdom and love of my wonderful grandparents, and the dream angels that made my sleep more peaceful. Love is a powerful thing.

Unlike many others sent to residential schools across Canada, my brothers and I never lost our first language. Nowadays, when talking to residential school survivors, people tell me, "I understand some and can say simple words and phrases but I can't speak my native language fluently anymore." Fortunately, for the native people living in the James Bay region, the Cree language remains strong, mainly because Anglican and Roman Catholic priests learned Cree before coming to the people, and here English and French language speakers have never outnumbered us.

Once September came, we were back at the residential school. My second year was very much like my first, except I had learned English, knew better how to stay out of trouble and/or not get caught. Like most Anglican-administered Indian Residential Schools, the emphasis at Pelican Lake was on the supremacy of white people, English, the King, and the church—and not always in that order.

Forced assimilation meant more than just residential schools. Our ancient cultural ceremonies were made illegal, and the Royal Canadian Mounted Police enforced the law. Police raided outlawed, traditional ceremonies, people were arrested, and drums and artifacts were destroyed.

I survived school by counting time using the white man's calendar. I knew that my time here would end and I would be going home.

When Reverend Marshall died on Christmas Eve, I pretended to be sad, but I was not. My friend Bertha and I decided that if Reverend Marshall was now in heaven, as they said he was, it was not the place where we wanted to go when we died. This presented us with a problem—"How to be bad without being caught and punished, so that when we died we would go to hell?" Hell seemed to be a better place than heaven with Reverend Marshal being there. Talks like this were always in the Cree language at the far end of the playground so that we would not to be overheard. I must tell you, that there were times when I felt as if I had shamed my spirit by being happy when Reverend Marshal died. Not anymore.

Wawahte—Peace in the Heavens

I later learned that the legend Papa told me walking home from Christmas Eve church service about the northern lights had also been told to other Cree children. I will never forget how we kids would all gather around and watch the Wawahte. When certain that we were alone and that no one else could hear us, we would speak in our beautiful Cree language telling each other things like: "There, see that one is the spirit of my Mama who died when I was little. She has come to dance for me. She is telling me to be strong and that she loves me." We would also ask the spirit angels to take dream letters to our parents and grandparents and to bring their dream letters back to us.

All mail to and from children was censored. Any mail written in "Indian" was destroyed. Basically, the only letters that we were allowed to send our parents were the lies that the teacher wrote on the blackboard and we copied as our own. There was no limit to our misery, yet in our own very special way we found moments of peace with Wawahte.

Although this was a very long time ago, I remember the tranquil feelings that came over me and the other children as we stood before our heavenly altar looking sky ward. We went to bed those nights with smiles on our faces and we slept well. The spirit angels had lifted us to our feet when our wings had trouble remembering how to fly.

Years later, I told my very religious Moochum about this and he said, "Child, that is how we are to feel by going to church." Regrettably, Reverend Marshall and his successor, Reverend Cheales, spoiled that for me.

Reverend Cheales, who became the school principal after Reverend Marshal died, came to Pagwa the following summer to pick up the kids for the train trip back to school. That night on the train, the seats in the coach were folded down and made into beds. I was sleeping on an outside seat next to the aisle and awoke screaming. The Canadian National Railroad passenger train conductor who had made the seats into beds was touching me in my private parts. This train conductor had sexually assaulted me, a nine-year-old girl. Reverend Cheales was in the train coach at the time, knew what had taken place and other than asking me, "Did that man hurt your back-side?" he took no action. I was never taken to see a doctor nor did anyone ask me about what had happened or acknowledge that I was assaulted [1].

Late in the winter, my Papa came to visit when my sister Greta was very ill and was left lying unattended in bed. I told Papa what was happening and he found her unconscious. Papa immediately had Greta flown to the Sioux Lookout hospital, in an airplane with skis, where he demanded that they care for her. She survived thanks only to Papa's actions.

My parents defied the rules after what had happened to Greta and to me on the train. They did not allow us to go back to school the following year. I endured seven years of Pelican Lake Indian Residential School's austere surroundings, exacting lessons, hard labour work details, and strict religious services. I saw the school for my last time in 1945. After all is said, I extend a very special thank you to the one kind supervisor/teacher, Miss Goodwin, who took us on outdoor excursions, affording us rare periods of mischievous fun and giving us freedom to speak our native language. Miigwetch Miss Goodwin, the children loved you.

My experience there has troubled me my entire life. I have been angry for what happened. I tried to understand why and how this happened to me, and the thousands of others who attended residential schools. We were made to feel ashamed of having been born Indian. That is why I, like many residential school survivors, have endured a lifetime of struggle. For many years, it was easier to allow myself to feel ashamed as if I were to blame. I now see the obstacle of our past as an opportunity to improve conditions for our people. We cannot change the past, but we are beginning to see one-another without some preconceived bias and have shown that we are able to live together in harmony with one-another. I now have many non-Aboriginal friends. More important, I no longer give a x@%& when someone gives me their "Indian straight out of the bush" look. It is their problem—not mine!

As awful as my school experience was, it taught me skills that I have used every day of my life. I learned to speak and read the English language, to cook, do needlework, and make quilts. Skills, that in reality, my own mother could have taught me had I gone to school in my village, and not 800 kilometers away. As a child, I also learned from my community how to live on the land; for this I will forever be thankful. Living on the land is not as easy as in times past.

I now know who and what I am and that I will no longer bow my head in defeat. I take pride in being a Canadian and living in one of the few countries in the world that promotes a multicultural society. Canada's official multiculturalism policy began in 1971. Immigrants and now Aboriginal people are no longer encouraged to fit a Euro-Canadian mold. People can be Canadian, and if they wish, rightfully honour their ancestral heritage; I am a Canadian-Cree, Canadian-German, etc. We are not a melting pot of different people but a society that draws its strength from peoples' differences. Unlike when I was a child, I am now optimistic that soon we will all have the opportunity to get the quality education needed to succeed in this highly complex and technical world. I have told you my story in the hope that young Aboriginals and other previously persecuted minorities will make the effort to become successful at whatever they choose to do. May the Great Spirit guide you!

Coming to the decision to tell my past was difficult. Once I began to open my heart and my soul, for all to see, much of my pain went away. The human heart has the ability to forgive but not to forget. Thank you for listening.

Esther and the log cabin quilt that she
completed in 2011

Quilting is truly a labour of love ... love for the memories in life, for the one intended and for the treasured craft that it is. Like nature, it takes both the big and the little pieces of fabric to tell the story. Humans have not woven the web of life. We are but one thread within it. Whatever we do to the web, we do to ourselves. All things are bound together all things are connected. Like my quilt the many pieces of fabric are sewed by different-coloured thread, as in nature all things are bound together. All things are connected.

———————————

Shattered Innocence: End Note:

1. In 2012 Esther was denied special compensation for her sexual assault claim, on the grounds that it occurred outside the premises of the school even though she was, at the time, under the care of the school officials.

Part Two

They Call Me Bunnie

I have been told it was the nuns at the Roman Catholic McIntosh Indian Residential School that began calling me Bunnie. This was because I was so small and darted about like a baby bunny rabbit. My parents named me Mary Elizabeth, but at the Residential School they had no record of me having been baptized, so they baptized me for a second time—Marie Louise. I answer to Bunnie!

I was born in 1936 to Frank and Phyllis Tenniscoe, who some years before my birth moved to northwestern Ontario from Golden Lake, an Algonquin reserve in southeastern Ontario. It is rumoured in the family they moved to Quetico, 155 kilometers down the Canadian National Railway west of Thunder Bay, since 1970 the unified Twin Cities of Fort William and Port Arthur, as the result of legal issues concerning my father's back east alcohol distilling

McIntosh Indian Residential School Bunnie at
two years of age

operation—back east he made moonshine. I say it is a
family rumour, as I have no childhood memories of my
parents. My father, unable to care for my sister Ruth and for
me, put us into the custody of the Roman Catholic nuns
at the McIntosh Indian Residential School. The school
was located at the southeast end of Canyon Lake near
Vermillion Bay, Ontario, at the Canadian National Railroad
stop of Quibell.

I was reluctant when first approached to reopen doors
to my past, not because school was a bad place, but because
it was growing up feeling cheated out of knowing my
family. Unlike the experiences of many Indian children

who attended residential schools, the nuns and staff treated Ruth and me with love and kindness. Telling my story has been a daunting experience—revisiting the haunting memories and emotions—but this has been good for me. For me, my anger at my parents for abandoning me, and my childhood feelings that I was to blame, were unhealthy and self-defeating. I now accept what happened, and understand I was not to blame.

I am also a visible minority Indian[1] woman—victim of our history's official policy of racism, once widely accepted and touted as beneficial. Change is on the horizon—we need to know of this dark chapter of history if we are to see the sun rise upon all Canadians thriving in greater human harmony. The future does not just happen—it is created. It is for this reason alone, that I tell my story.

I was born in destitute times. It was the Great Depression. This was a time, especially difficult, for Indian people, particularly for parents like mine with large families. My parents were very poor and there were many of us living in a two-room shack in the bush alongside a lake and the railway tracks. There was no work close to home for my father, nor was there any kind of social assistance from the province or the Department of Indian Affairs. The furbearing animal populations were reduced to near extinction due to poverty, high fur prices, and competitive over-trapping.

Though Aboriginal life was once in harmony with nature: wildlife conservation and environmental protection are not the indulgences of impoverished hungry people.

My father was desperate for work, desperate for a means to survive, and for that reason left the older children in the care of relatives, and took my two-year-old sister Ruth and one-year-old me, with them for summer work 35 miles north of Kenora, Ontario. My father said, "The wolf was at our door. I needed to do something desperate to keep from losing my summer job guiding fishermen for Minaki Lodge." When my mother was in hospital giving birth to my brother Louis, my father realized that he would be unable to care for us without losing his job. Unknown to my mother, he gave the two of us into the care of the nuns at the Residential School. How could she have ever forgiven him? I still question why they never came back for us; we waited and waited . . . Ruth and I, orphaned by our parents, never got to go home summers.

McIntosh Indian Residential School opened in 1924 and burned to the ground on the 19th of March 1965. My sister Ruth and I were there continuously, from 1937 until 1948. Unlike what so many say about how bad their treatment was and the deplorable conditions, I was loved, well cared for, and not abused, except for the occasional well-deserved spanking. Child spanking was then highly recommended by the guide as to how to properly rear children. The motto of the day was "Spare the rod and spoil the child."

I have now twice said that I was loved, and you might ask what makes me believe that. I know it to be so, not because I was fed well and clothed, but because the nuns, the priest, and the staff at the school had time for me. I learned from them, my caregivers, how to show love and when my sons Rocky and René were born I knew how to demonstrate my love for them. I once heard it said, "To a child, love is spelled T-I-M-E." I was a good mother, and yes, I occasionally stick-trained my boys, but only when it became a matter of their safety. Little boys have a way of putting themselves in real danger when they live beside lakes and rivers.

My first childhood memory is of a nun, who was not wearing her habit, picking me up out of my bed and comforting me after I had a bad dream. I had been ill and was sleeping in the small adjacent room off the nun's bedroom where I had slept when I was a baby. The nun's bedroom door opened into the little kids' dormitory. Babies and sick children, needing to be watched more closely, slept in the "little room."

My older sisters, Jeanie, Florence, Rose-Marie eventually joined during the school year and we all became close, but Ruth and I were especially close.

I attended class, had duties that I sometimes did not like, and learned skills that I have since used every day of my life. I also added both the French and Anishinabek (Ojibwa) languages to my command of English. The language of the school was English; I learned French from listening to the French Canadian nuns talking between themselves and I learned Anishinabek from the other children. I have no recollection of children being disciplined for speaking their native languages while at play or in their dormitory. We spoke English in the classroom, on work detail, while in church, and at mealtime. I am told that although my parents spoke Algonquin, they never taught it to my brothers and sisters who lived at home. Being punished for speaking "Indian" was something I learned about years after I left school.

Upon leaving school in 1948, I went back to live with my parents for a short time, but this did not work because I did not fit in well with their family life. After a few weeks, I went to live with my sister Jeanie and her husband Phillip Sawdo, a W.W. II war hero, who owned and operated a fly-in fishing lodge on Sanford Lake north of Atikokan in northwestern Ontario. It was there that I learned about life in the Canadian bush. Phillip and Jeanie, with their small children at their side, constructed a lodge, cabins, docks, and service buildings on what was undeveloped lake shoreline. The only way in was by boat and portaging or airplane.

If something needed doing, they did it themselves. It was here that I learned how to fish, hunt, cook, and care for the Americans who came in the summer to fish. I also learned from Phillip and Jeanie the skills of trapping and how to survive in the bush. And, surviving in the bush brings me to Joe.

It was here that I met Joe Kries, who became my first husband when I was seventeen years old, and the father of my two sons. Joe, who had recently emigrated from the country of Luxembourg in Europe, was working in a nearby lumber camp. Joe loved the bush life; although a blacksmith by trade, his life was hunting and trapping. The photograph below is my man Joe, his dog Charley, and the building with the smoke coming out of the chimney is where we lived. One cold winter's day when all was as still as the moon, and I, God-forbid, complained about the miles and miles of isolation, Joe replied: "Why? It is only a seven-mile walk through the bush to the railroad tracks." I thought best, not to mention, when at the "railroad tracks" one was left with another 160 kilometers to see people, visit stores, eat a meal you did not cook yourself, or have ice cream.

If there was ever a person that was truly a wannabe Indian, it was Joe. Sadly, he drowned one August while towing a canoe behind a powerboat on Baril Lake, near Owakonze, Ontario.

My man, my dog, and my home

I now live in Thunder Bay, with my second husband of thirty-five years, Garry Galvin. Looking back on my seventy-five years, there have been many tripping sticks and stones along the path of life. There were good times, bad times, and times I choose not to think about. When I stumbled, I got up, shook myself off, and went on to a better day. I have a great but normally dysfunctional family of eighteen brothers and sisters, two wonderful sons, and a lifetime of good friends from both the Aboriginal and non-Aboriginal communities. I cherish my First Nation heritage as my sons treasure both their Aboriginal and European ancestry. I have learned to become self-confident and I am completely comfortable in both cultures. I like to say that I now walk with a moccasin on one foot and a high-heeled shoe on the other, admittedly a bit awkward at times. These awkward moments come mostly from people within the Indian community who imply that I am not "Indian" enough. I have become my own person, a person with pride who no longer blames others for her own shortcomings.

I am also forever grateful that I had an opportunity to go to school. My brother Richard never did. Realizing the importance of becoming educated, Richard began grade one at the age of thirty. He was driven to learn to read and write so that he could apply for jobs that he knew he could do but for which he would not be hired because he was unable to complete the job application. Over the years he took advantage of adult education programs, completing high school after he suffered a stroke that caused the left side of his body to be mostly paralyzed. Then, unable to continue working as a heavy equipment operator, Richard and his wife, Carman, purchased a Chinese food restaurant that they have successfully run in Grande Cache, Alberta, for many years. Richard, as your proud sister, I ask that you accept these words as a symbolic eagle feather that you place in your bonnet of achievements. Please continue to tell our youth that without an education you could have never been a heavy equipment operator or a successful businessman.

Some years ago I began to be concerned about my heritage and what history had done to First Nations. I re-established my Indian status, as defined by the Indian Act, and transferred my band registration to Lac Des Mille Lacs First Nation. My primary concern is how to make our future better than our past. There is no way that we can rewrite history and all go back to living on the land as we once did. There is no real future for us individually and culturally unless we become socially and economically a part of mainstream society. The Residential School legacy continues to affect people and is a problem that will not easily go away.

Upon leaving school, I too lived with demons and ghosts, which I would have to learn to deal with. My fears were different than those of many residential school survivors, and their progeny, who continue to suffer from past experiences. My ghosts were ghosts of me being abandoned by my parents and believing that it must have been my fault. In hindsight, I see being at McIntosh School as a blessing. There I was not bullied, as so many were elsewhere, by a system that treated "Indian" children with contempt. I have no recall of ever going to bed hungry or having to do without the necessities of life. Nevertheless, I had to face up to the fact that I was not a reject to be discarded. Thankfully, I had the good fortune of an environment of belonging and acceptance giving me the confidence to tell myself that I was a worthwhile person, and the ghosts slowly went away never to return.

The legacy of Canada's Indian residential school system needs to be understood and addressed if we, as a nation, are to move forward. Learning and knowing about our history is a prerequisite to our healing and reconciliation of today and the restoration of our families and culture. The future does not just happen—it is created. It is now our turn, not to be confrontational, but to walk proud as equals in Canadian society.

All I have to do is look to my two sons, Rocky and René, to know that life does not need to be one of despair and personal failure. Knowing that the life-blood of my boys' success was their self-discipline and self-motivation, I saw it to be my parental obligation to support their dreams. I encouraged them to become educated and to be comfortable interacting with the broader Canadian society, while at the same time being cemented in their own identity. I now look upon the two of them with pride for what they have made of their lives. My eldest, Rocky, retired in February 2011, at age 56, as Director General, National Operations Services Systems, for the Department of Human Resources Development Canada. René, after serving in the Canadian Forces, chose to live in the bush where he has been employed year-round for many years at a youth camp. Not bad for a couple of kids that got their start growing up on the trap-line!

Although Joe and I did our utmost to shield our two boys from the cruelty of racial discrimination, the boys, too had their problems with those who sneered at them as "half-breeds." It then should come as no surprise that my hero is Reverend Doctor Martin Luther King Jr. His famous words, "I have a dream that my four little children will one day live in a nation where they will not be judged by the color of their skin, but by the content of their character."

These words remind us that having values is important, but living them is much more important, and that words without deeds are nothing. A single person can express in words a vision for all mankind, but it takes the commitment of millions of the masses to make that vision a reality. I share this poem written by Rocky shortly after Dr. King's assassination as my young son expressing his personal pain with racism:

In Memory of a Great Man
Rocky Kries, Grade VII
St. Patrick's School
(April 1968)

Dr. King was a great one in our land
Until he died by a gunman's hand
Of his colour, he was proud.
He spoke with a voice crisp and loud
For one race his life he gave.

A single bullet brought the end
While grieving many a friend
For his death he was prepared
And for his family he cared
One single life he had to give
So one mighty race could live.

Many of his policies did make sense
Especially one of non-violence
And many a good speech he made
before into grave he was laid
For God he had love
And now he may be in heaven above.

Things in his life varied
Until the day he was buried

His massive funeral ceremony
Held its rhythm and harmony
He left the nation in pain
While in the grave he was laid.

He fought for what was right
To bring a race into light
He held but one aim
To destroy Negro poverty and shame
Only one goal he set
Until with tragedy he met.

His death stunned the world
And flags at half-mast unfurled
He stood straight and tall
And held no fear at all
To this man, a lot we owe
His death dealt us a mighty blow.
The end

It is with great sadness that I see Aboriginal and non-Aboriginal youth, with such great potential, struggling with issues that keep them from becoming competitively educated. For many First Nation cultures, education is not the same as the regimentation of a formal schooling. Historically, as parents, we did not make demands of our children to learn. Now some find it difficult to provide the parental support children need to successfully acquire an education. Too many children do not know their own culture or their own country.

There are people in our community who say that the white man's schools are no good and Indian children should not go to them. They do not mean this, but native-based-and-delivered education continues to be substandard to mainstream, provincially administered schooling in Canada. This I believe to be something that requires immediate and thoughtful change. As First Nation people, we cannot continue doing as we have done and expect a different outcome. The political pendulum has swung in our favour and we must cease trying to change the past and earnestly and accountably create a new and better future for ourselves and in the process for all Canadians.

We need to provide standardized education to all our youth and ensure that those children who succeed scholastically become the celebrated leaders, of our communities. It is our children's educations, I symbolize here, with an imaginary gift of sweet grass braid to bring a harmony that shall never be broken.

"Mamonpiimoosaywin"[2] (Walking Forward Together)

Mequietch/Thank You, *Bunnie*

They Call Me Bunnie: End Notes:

1. Bunnie holds to the term "Indian."

2. Oji-Cree Language—The Oji-Cree people are descended from historical intermarriage between the Ojibwa and Cree cultures, but are generally considered a distinct nation from either of their parent groups.

Part Three

Elder Stanley Stephens

A Man of Principle
"As Long as the River Flows, Grass Grows
and Sun Shines"

I was born September 1939 to Cree parents Alex and Bella Stephens in a tent on my family's traditional hunting and trapping area located not far from Mammamattawa Village, Esther's childhood home. Until I was eight years old, my mother, father, sister, grandparents, and uncle spent the fall and winter months on our trapping area, returning to the village early each year before the spring breakup. After all these years, I still remember the excitement and wonderful sight of the geese returning and the sounds the river made as it cleared itself of ice. The spring breakup was nature's promise that summer was not far off.

In 1945, like many families living in Mammamattawa Village, my parents were told that their children must go to school, so we moved one hundred kilometers up-river to Pagwa River Village. There, my father and I, with the help of family and community, built a small log house. We went up the river about two kilometers to cut the logs that we towed back to the village behind our canoe. Building a permanent house was in itself a great adventure, as none of my family had ever lived in anything but traditional shelters made from tree bark and animal hides, then later, canvas tent houses purchased from the Hudson's Bay Trading Post. Our little log house had an upstairs where we kids slept. Interesting to note, my Moochum went his whole life having never slept in a bed—traditionally our people slept on the ground.

My friend, Esther, has often asked why she and other native children were made to attend residential school while others went to the village day school. Unfortunately time has erased the particulars and I no longer remember why my sister Jemima and I were not sent to a residential school. At the time, the Indian Act stipulated that the decision to allow an "Indian" child to attend a community day school was that of the local Indian Agent [1].

From what I now recall, many aspects of my day school experience were not unlike those children who attended residential schools. I remember well becoming aware that I was an "Indian" in a rather painful manner. I entered grade one in the Pagwa Village day school at the age of eight and had some traumatic experiences because speaking Cree, the only language my family spoke, was taboo at school. Within my first 15 minutes at school I was strapped six times on each hand with a heavy leather strap for speaking "Indian." Not only was I not allowed to speak my own language on school property, but also like other Aboriginal children I was subjected to methodical abuse from teachers whose role it was to quash, or so it seemed, to beat the Indian out of us. School was something my sister Jemima and I had looked forward to with excitement. My hands were so swollen from my first day's strapping that I was unable to hold a pencil for a week. It took me much longer for the emotional wound to heal. Then there were the icy stares from the teacher while the rest of the class would, with the teacher's approval, roar with laughter whenever I attempted to speak English or participate in anything academic. These childhood experiences did not give me a good feeling about being Aboriginal. There was no attempt by teachers or the school administration to understand or accommodate native children's cultural differences, let alone understand how we were taught to learn differently from Euro-Canadian children.

I remember asking a ten-year-old Anishinabek boy if he skated. He answered, "Yes, but I don't have skates and I have never really skated." I gave the boy a pair of skates. He then put them on and skated for his first time—not all that well, but he knew the moves and he was able not only to skate forward, but also backwards. How was this possible? He had learned to skate as he had learned most everything else he knew—by observation. At the risk of labelling people, the Cree and Anishinabek are historically indirect cultures and do not learn through the direct act of being taught specifically how to do something. But rather, Cree and Anishinabek children traditionally learned by watching and by peer—and Elder praise, first for having the courage to try and then for succeeding.

This early stage of painful self-discovery, involving my ethnic background, continued to have a negative influence in my early life. Eventually I came to realize that I must reject my negative feelings about having been born "Indian," not white, and become my own person. My father, like any parent, was not perfect, but he was a great friend and role model. I learned both from his strengths and shortcomings. He was strong of will, honest, and a dependable provider. On occasion, he also drank too much alcohol and became abusive and did things he otherwise would not do. Both his positive and his negative manner were good influences for me, as were my family and our community Elders. Through them I came to the realization that I had to become proud of who I was before I could become strong and move on with my life. My father and the Elders got me to understand that I, Stanley, am responsible for my own future. Their vision of our future was obvious. Those of us who left the land to live in permanent community housing, and work by the wemistikoskiw calendar and clock, would struggle to fit socially and economically into that world. Without a doubt, my generation was a transitional generation. The Elder's long-ago soft-spoken words ring true; we experienced, and we continue to experience, profound cultural, economic, and political change.

In 1951, when I was twelve years old, my family moved from Pagwa to what is now Constance Lake Indian Reserve where my father took a job in a nearby sawmill and we moved into Department of Indian Affairs Reserve housing. The story of Pagwa, like that of most of Canada's north, is a story of jobs. When there were no longer enough jobs in Fort Albany, people moved to Mammamattawa Village, and when there were no jobs there people moved to Pagwa. By 1950, Mammamattawa Village was mostly deserted. In time, many people then moved from Pagwa in search of employment.

The Constance Lake Indian Reserve day school proved to be better than the school in Pagwa, and I was able to complete grade six. Looking back, I now think that going to school on the Reserve was better because I was not being bullied by a system that treated "Indian" children with contempt. Instead, my teacher, Mr. Jefferies, went to a great effort relating textbook learning to the happenings of our day-to-day life. Other teachers conducted classroom demonstrations showing us the meaning of what was written in our textbooks. We went on field trips that focused on linking textbook theory with observation in the real world. As a little kid I had the feeling that my teachers liked me and wanted all of us to do well in school.

This was at a time when achieving more than a grade eight education was not perceived to be a prerequisite for employment. The Indian Act prohibited "Indian" children from going to school beyond the age of sixteen, lessening their chances of finding a good job. Unlike many of my peer group, who dropped out of school and turned to alcohol, I saw the value of an education. In the mid-1960s, through a Canada Manpower adult education program in Sudbury, Ontario, I went on to high school. From my father, I learned the skills of hunting and trapping and I worked alongside him cutting pulpwood and doing other manual work.

When making a living by trapping was no longer possible and there was no work in the bush, I took a series of jobs in Kenora and Winnipeg, working for the railroad. I did this for one year, until I became lonesome for home.

So in 1961, I returned home to Constance Lake Indian Reserve, now known as Constance Lake First Nation, where I got married, raised a family, and have lived since. When our first house was being built, I did all the insulation, dry walling, windows, and painting myself. Growing up, my father counselled that: "Learn the pride that comes from doing for yourself." Doing much of the work building our family home created in me a sense of pride even though Indian Affairs in Ottawa actually owned the house. The Indian Act prohibits people living on Indian Reserves to hold ownership title to their homes or to the land they occupy.

My lifetime job résumé will show that I have done many kinds of work. I have served several terms on the Band Council of Constance Lake First Nation and I served one term as Chief. Of all my jobs, none have been more gratifying than being a Canadian Forces Ranger for the last ten years. Currently I am a Master Corporal. The following, taken from the Canadian Forces website, describes the Ranger program:

Canadian Rangers

The Canadian Rangers, a sub-component of the Canadian Forces Reserve, provide patrols and detachments for employment on national-security and public-safety missions in those sparsely settled northern, coastal and isolated areas of Canada, which cannot conveniently or economically be covered by other elements or components of the Canadian Forces. Formally established in 1947, the Canadian Rangers protect Canada's sovereignty by reporting unusual activities or sightings, collecting local data of significance to the Canadian Forces, and conducting surveillance or sovereignty patrols as required.

Canadian Rangers are dedicated, knowledgeable members of the Army and reflect the diversity of the communities they belong to. Many Canadian Rangers are Aboriginal and there are a total of 23 different languages spoken. Easily recognized by their red sweatshirts and ball caps, the Canadian Rangers play an important role in advancing public recognition of Canada's Inuit, First Nations and Métis.

There are currently over 4,250 Canadian Rangers in 169 communities across Canada. This number is expected to increase to 5,000 in 2012.

What has made being a Ranger so appealing to me is that I am not only doing something worthwhile for my country but that I work with many of our young people. I am able to teach them, and members of Canada's military, winter survival skills and bush field craft, things I learned as a youth. As Rangers we stand ready to assist in time of emergency. The mission of the Canadian Rangers is "to provide lightly equipped, self-sufficient, mobile forces in support of the

Canadian Forces' sovereignty and domestic operation tasks in Canada." I was very proud to have been presented with the Ranger Special Service Medal by Lieutenant-General Andrew Leslie at a ceremony in 2006 in Ottawa.

Lieutenant-General Andrew Leslie, Chief of
Land Staff, and Ranger Master Corporal
Stanley Stephens

Aboriginal "Indian" War Veterans

For the last several years I have been an active member of the Royal Canadian Legion where I help organize community events in honour of Canada's war veterans—in particular Aboriginal war veterans. Examples of the bravery and commitment of Aboriginal veterans are as follows:

- "From the Battle of Queenston Heights in the War of 1812, up through World War I (1914-1918),

World War II (1939-1945) and the Korean War (1950-1953), Aboriginal people have fought long and hard, volunteering en masse for active duty, despite being exempt from Canadian conscription laws. It is estimated that 4,000 men gave of themselves to fight in the Great War. Many natives living in some of Canada's most remote areas, enlisted with great personal effort. One man by the name of William Semice walked from Lake St. Joseph to what is now Thunder Bay in order to enlist. This was a distance of over 800 kilometers. John Campbell, another patriotic native, travelled 4,800 kilometers to Vancouver by a combination of trail, canoe, and river steamer to enlist in the Canadian Expeditionary Force so he could fight in W.W.I." (*The Indian News*, 1970, Vol. 13, No. 8, p. 3).

- A generation of young Aboriginal Canadian men bravely fought on the battlefields of Europe during World War I. Approximately 300 of them never returned home. When Canada declared war on Germany on September 10, 1939, the "Indian" community once again responded quickly. Four years later, in May 1943, the government declared that, as British subjects, all able "Indian" men of military age could be called up for training and service in Canada or overseas (Summerby, 1993, p.-21). Therefore, in direct contrast to World War I, most "Indians" were not exempt from conscription. By this time, however, many Aboriginals had already volunteered for overseas duty.

• "Indians" volunteered to fight in the air, on land, or on the high seas including those who fought in submarines. During the first three years of the war, enlistment was made difficult by racism. The air force had stipulated that all recruits "<u>shall</u>" be of "pure European descent" and the Royal Canadian Navy required applicants to "be a British born subject, of a White Race" (Gaffen, 1985, p. 64). Max Basque, an "Indian" from Whycocomagh, experienced this racism. As a former merchant marine Max travelled to Montreal to enlist in the Canadian Navy:

• The Navy recruiting officer looked at me. He said, "Are you an Indian?" I said, "Yes, sir." "Sorry we don't take 'Indians' in the Navy. But . . . you're not a full-blooded Indian." "No I'm not," I said. "I don't think there are any full-blooded Indians east of Winnipeg! . . . But on the books I'm an Indian. Here's my border-crossing card." You know, we used to carry those "I am an Indian cards." "Well," he said, "you got a French name: B-a-s-q-u-e. We'll sign you as a Frenchman." I said, "No, you won't . . . That's not a French name, anyway. It's Basque . . .

it's from northern Spain." "Well," he said, "we'll sign you on as Basque." I said, "No. On the books, I was born on the Indian reserve and I've always gone as an Indian all my life . . . What in the world? Disown my own race, just to get into the Navy?" I said, "I'm a Canadian, even if I am an Indian. Same as you are . . . I was born here in Canada." Max Basque never did join the Canadian Navy. (*Cape Breton's Magazine*, No. 52, p. 58)

Though racism was for some an issue during enlistment, combat made all soldiers brothers. Unfortunately public policy changed that upon military discharge. Aboriginal veterans were excluded from receiving land grants given to non-native veterans because the Indian Act did not allow "Indians" to own title to land. At war's end, a few veterans like Lance Corporal Paudash managed to put the pain of war behind them and move on to a better and productive life . . .

Lance Corporal Johnston Paudash:

Lance Corporal Johnston Paudash was a much-decorated sniper in WWI. He was credited with 42 enemy kills and decorated by King George V for bravery in the field. Living in Lindsay, Ontario, Johnston, on his own initiative crossed

Canada and the United States numerous times while assembling exhibits in support of Indian Treaty claims. At the government's request, Johnston attended the 1923 sitting in Ottawa where inquiries into the treatment of Indians were held. On his death, Premier Frost called for a moment of silence in the Ontario Parliament in recognition of both his military service and his dedication to his people (A Chambers Family, pp. 55 and 56; Copyright © 2011).

For all too many, the lives of war heroes became something closer to that of Tommy Prince.

Thomas George "Tommy" Prince:

Tommy Prince was one of Canada's most decorated First Nation soldiers, serving in both World War II and the Korean War. Growing up, Tommy became a superb marksman with exceptional tracking skills learned from countless days spent hunting in the Manitoba wilderness around his Brokenhead Indian Reserve.

At the outbreak of World War II, Tommy volunteered to fight with the Canadian Army and although he easily met the requirements for recruitment, he was turned down several times before he was finally accepted on June 3, 1940. He was promoted to Sergeant in 1942, when his Canadian Parachute Battalion merged with American units, later to be called the Devil's Brigade. In 1945, Tommy was ordered to Buckingham Palace where King George VI presented him with his Military Medal, including the Silver Star on behalf of U.S. President Roosevelt, for his battlefield bravery near Littoria, Italy, in February 1944. In all, he was decorated nine times, the most of any Aboriginal soldier in World War II. Honourably discharged on June 15, 1945, Tommy returned to civilian life later to re-enlist in the Canadian Army in 1950 to fight with United Nations troops in the Korean War. Tommy, once again, was decorated for his battlefield skill and bravery.

Adjusting to civilian life was not easy for Tommy after his years of service. Discrimination, pain of war, old war wounds, and arthritic knees, as the result of long harsh conditions during his military service, coupled with alcoholism resulted in Tommy's final years being spent virtually alone.

He lived in a Salvation Army hostel. In order to support himself, he sold off his medals.

War hero Tommy Prince died 1977 at Deer Lodge Hospital in Winnipeg and was interred in the Brookside Cemetery.

Lance Corporal Johnston Paudash and Sergeant Thomas George "Tommy" Prince— you made us proud.

Anti-Sealing Movement kills our way of Life

I still hold a license to a Registered Trap Line but now I only trap as a hobby and to show young people how we once lived and earned a living. Over the centuries our native culture evolved into a respectful relationship with wildlife and nature. I was taught from an early age that upon taking the life of an animal, I should reverently pause and thank the Creator as well as the animal for giving its life so our people could live. I was also taught that it was wrong to mutilate or waste the flesh of an animal, and that disrespecting nature would result in terrible consequences.

In 1969, the International Fund for Animal Welfare began to mobilize public opinion against the annual hunt of baby harp seals off Canada's east coast. Other animal welfare groups, including Greenpeace, protested against what they perceived as the savage, uncontrolled slaughter of helpless baby Harp seals for their white pelts. Like many well-meaning people, I supported the animal welfare movement whose aim it was to end the seal hunt. I was horrified seeing pictures of baby seals being clubbed, and then being skinned while still moving. It was not the killing of the baby seal that troubled me but the disrespectful way in which it was done. In the end, our well-meaning intentions and the deceptive business practices of animal rights organizations ended in another setback to our way of life.

The anti-seal hunt movement cleverly used well-known, mostly female, movie celebrities to publicize "the bloody barbaric hunt," building up their financial and worldwide public support to what was being portrayed as "grisly slaughter" of baby Harp seals. One such celebrity was Brigitte Bardot, who reportedly never set foot on the ice floes where the white-coated baby seals are whelped. Her poster child photograph clutching a baby seal was reportedly taken with a taxidermy-mounted baby Harp seal in France. What began as the "kill the seal hunt movement" very quickly generated enormous amounts of money and soon it became a successful advocate to end the wearing of all natural furs. The anti-fur movement's argument was not scientifically based but rather capitalized on human emotion. Government and professional wildlife management were powerless in the face of the parade of "cleavage scientists" who found their way to European rule makers and the western fashion industry that once championed wild-caught fur. The consequence was that people who once earned their living trapping went from middle class to demoralizing poverty. For a great many Natives, as well as others, the effects of this went well beyond economic loss. It was difficult to believe how quickly the change came. People went from economically being middle class to a life of dependence on social assistance. Gone also were the family building blocks of personal pride, the teaching tools of a strong work ethic, and environmental responsibility that for centuries measured and made us who we were.

When the wild fur industry all but died in the 1970s so did our economic means to an independent life. Yes, forced assimilation and residential schools were and continue to be the cause of a great amount of social dysfunction in our society, but so has been the disappearance of family-based fur trapping, as we knew it.

The fur industry is now beginning to murmur its way back. Time, a decline in the adverse, kill-the-seal-hunt, media hype, changes to Newfoundland's method of harvesting seals, Asian wealth, and fur-harvester co-ops have given cause for some old trappers to go in search of their snowshoes. Canada's first product export, wild-fur, is once again in demand. North Bay Fur Harvesters Auction, North America's second biggest, operates as a unique co-op of Aboriginal and non-Aboriginal trappers. About thirty species of wild animal hides from some 7,000 harvesters draw three hundred and more international fur buyers to the auction annually. International fur buyers come mostly from China, Denmark, Russia, Greece, and the United States four times a year to buy Canadian fur. Now that fur is once more in demand, better prices are being paid to trappers.

The resurgence of a fur industry for many First Nation people is good, but I do not suggest that the lives of First Nation people will be as they were in the past. With the collapse of the fur industry, most Aboriginal people were forced to give up their traditional way of life and as a result lost their identity and connection to the land.

No longer needing to cut wood, carry water, hunt, and gather food led to idleness, loss of purpose and self-worth, substance abuse, and family dysfunction. Likewise, the once self-reliant and family-engaged youth, now no longer having survival responsibility, turned to gang culture and became alienated from family and Elders' respect. Many of our young people today never experience the personal pride that I felt when I snared my first fox. Wow! This was a family moment of pride, me a little boy of eight making a financial contribution to the family. Then there was the time I shot my first moose as a teenager. I was treated as if I had won the Stanley Cup—meat for family and community. In the past, getting one's first rifle or shotgun—or undertaking one's first hunting expedition—was a common and exciting rite of passage. To hunt is to become an adult, where the principles of respect and conservation are passed down from generation to generation.

Although hunting remains an important part of some Native lives today, times have now changed and we must cultivate different ways to celebrate our youth on their way to becoming responsible adults.

Esther, Bunnie, and I are mere traces of a people impacted by generations of repressive social engineering.

What is important is that we give our voice to our unique perspective of history and that we go forth to seek peace after a conflict. We are not three people who will be written about in the history books; we tell our own uniquely intimate experience of history. We are First Nation people, so that by definition, our being here in Canada is different. We are unlike the people who have come to make their homes in multicultural Canada. We are people that from the beginning evolved culturally to survive by living in harmony with nature. Victims of generations of cultural genocide, many of us now strive to rediscover our heritage at a time when people worldwide struggle to become inclusive in worldwide technologies and economies. First Nation people not only struggle individually, but collectively, for Canadian cultural and economic inclusion and although much well—meaning determination and money has been invested to make it so, we face challenges that money alone will not solve. I once shared in the misconception that if we were given more money and free rein, all could be fixed. But I now realize all Canadians must have a hold on the reins too, and steer our country on a better course. We are united through environment, democracy, economy, and our health needs. For that reason, I restate what has already been said and submit that the following is a major tripping-stick along the path to bringing about positive change.

The first of the colonial forefathers' many, many sins was their declaration that their newly acquired subjects were to be exiled far out of sight on isolated reserves, and made dependent upon the good will of the greater society. And for this act of "generosity" we, the "Indians," were to be beholden to them as our benefactors. However, it was the establishment of the residential school system that said Aboriginals were incapable of good parenthood and their children must be taken from them. Is there any greater insult? Generations were robbed of the opportunity to learn parenthood or to experience the love of family and children. These are people forced by tyranny to surrender their culture to the new masters' way. As Phil Fontaine, Grand Chief of the Assembly of First Nations said in May 2007, "We have a right to be frustrated, concerned, and angry."

This is not to say that the present efforts of government and native leadership should be abandoned and new measures be drafted. There are numerous well-meaning and worthwhile initiatives toward resolving outstanding land claims and resolving the social and economic disparity of Canada's first people. But poverty and ignorance, while they aggravate recent discontent, are not the main causes. History has shown that people often have greater tolerance for injury than for insult. Money alone will not cure a political travesty.

In the past, some First Nation leadership may have coped with having their culture relegated to last place behind mainstream society. I sense that the rank and file are awakening to the realization that even some of their leaders have become like those with whom they deliberate, more interested in concentrating their power base and keeping the cash flowing, than resolving historical injustice. Short—and long-term appeasement strategies are little more than scams, rides on airplanes for more talk, and another crisis in the circle of life. This is a dangerous path to be on, as everyone loses. There is an urgent need for a new way forward if humanity is going to move towards a safer, sustainable future.

I believe that for us to have a successful journey forward, we must not allow our canoes to become stuck in the turbulent waters that long ago passed under the bridge. Historically, unjust social policies were based on politically correct values of that time. Aboriginal people worldwide were considered savages and as a result annihilated, enslaved, and subjected to abuses by colonization. These unforgivable acts judged by today's values were morally wrong but judgment without knowing the social and economic values of times past may very well hinder our struggle to move forward. We, as Canada's first people, hold the policies of forced integration and the Indian Residential school program in moral social contempt but so do most Canadians, except that most of them know little about the topic. Those of a more recent immigrant background have their own issues and problems and probably don't really care what happened at the founding of Canada. Public awareness and action are the challenge. We can and do accept the apologies of today's government and church representatives for the past.

I think that we, in general, appreciate that the Government of Canada and the churches have financially compensated residential school survivors for the wrongs committed by their predecessors. Ongoing community-based survivor reconciliation programs should continue, and services and help should be made available to victims old and new. I salute the Canadian justice system for now aggressively prosecuting those people who formerly escaped justice for sexually abusing our children.

I am proud to honour the talking stick tradition of my people. I tell my story and reveal my thoughts to honour my people, all Canadians and myself. It is now time for all to emerge from our cocoons and listen to the truths. Long gone are the days depicted in the 1940s Western movies romanticizing out-gunned, screaming Indians attacking settler wagon trains in defiant attempts to protect their territory. These cowboy and Indian movie scripts always concluded with the good and powerful, "God on their side" cowboys winning, and the savage Indians losing. We are no longer that inarticulate "Indian" of the past used to sell movie scripts, newspapers, and novels by lying elitists who demonize the Aboriginal and tell stories of the kidnappings of pretty little Christian white girls. This sophisticated bullying of the past haunts us to this day.

The clock of time only moves forward. Yet by studying the consequences of the Indian residential schools' forced assimilation we can gain the understanding needed to fit Aboriginal cultural identity into the broader Canadian society of today. Unlike what has happened in the past, our words and actions must be straightforward and honest—a rarity in the politically correct world of today.

To my Aboriginal brothers and sisters, I say, heed the wise words of National Chief of the Assembly of First Nations Shawn A-In-Chut Atleo's Grandmother who said, on June 11, 2008, as she and her grandson watched Prime Minister Stephen Harper apologize before the House of Commons, "Grandson, they are beginning to see us."

There are few First Nation families that have not been affected by trans-generational impact damage from past Indian Residential School experiences. Dysfunctional behaviour passed down from generation to generation dating back to parent and grandparents who were damaged by residential school experiences and because of this, perpetuated how life should not be. This is not to say that many have not shown the courage to be different, but for many it is the same never-ending story of alcoholism, drugs, domestic violence, and jail time.

Changing how we think about ourselves and how we live rests with the individual, but the tools of change need to be community based. We have the tools to fix problems, but do we have the courage to take a true account of ourselves and to move on from what has failed and invest in the new and different? This may not be easy but it may be the only way we have. First on the list, I believe we must focus on the importance of education and the need to bring First Nation schooling up to provincial standards. Second, teaching the history of Canada's indigenous peoples should be made a requirement.

I don't see the social problems that many First Nation communities now face as all process and problem solving. The best solutions will come out of conversations. When you are in a community and meeting people who struggle with the effects of post-generational impact caused by decades of forced integration and residential schools, it is hard not to maintain moral outrage. That is why we must sit together, exchange ideas, and learn from one another how to design social programs to move us forward from the community level upward. Whether we believe or not that we have all been created to bring about an ever-better world, the people of the world will not, and do not, stand still. What better way, then, for a discussion of how the places where we live help shape who and what we are, and what we may become?

Treasure seekers and their Christian missionary partners coming to the new world mistakenly thought it their imperial and Christian duty to instruct Aboriginals in the message and customs of European values and ways. They completely ignored the value of Aboriginal cultures. They were ignorant of the importance of unity in diversity—that people of different cultures, traditions, and lifestyles are still worthy of recognition. Their ways are not defective, just because they are ignorant of some latter-day philosophy or religion. Let us not, in turn, err in the same way. The problems that First Nations now face are not theirs alone. They are the problems of all Canadians and it will take the collective wisdom of all to ensure that all are brought along on our journey forward based on the principle that there is "unity–in–diversity."

Canada's multicultural policy is unique in the countries of the world. Likewise, so are First Nations and First Nation people unique in Canada. Unlike people who immigrated from elsewhere, Aboriginal people still have a claim to certain lands, resources, and compensations as set out in early treaties made with the Crown. Treaty rights, ignored for many years, are now being challenged through negotiation and court arbitration. Though many issues have been resolved, many long-standing grievances remain.

Unlike in the past, First Nations are now being consulted in the approval process for many development initiatives across Canada. First Nation consultation ranges in scope from forest operations, hydro development, mineral, oil and gas extraction, pipe and hydroelectric transmission lines, fishing, hunting, and most things that impact First Nations. Development proponents often find it extremely frustrating when attempting to do business with First Nations and they question why. Not to over-generalize, first among the difficulties experienced in doing business with First Nations is the issue of trust. From the time the first Europeans came to the new world, Indians were deceived, treated with disrespect, and made to stand back and watch Mother Earth being desecrated. The challenge in doing business with my people is not for you to make us see the good in what you are proposing, but to convince us that you can be trusted. You must also respect our right to say "No" when the cost to the environment outweighs short-term financial benefit.

The beautiful meaning behind the words "unity in diversity" will not come to be unless there is trust and mutual respect between all people. Humanity must embrace the intangibles of life—honour, family, community, and living space—more than money and positions of power. Begin by honouring yourself and aspire to have the common sense of a goose:

Do we have as much sense as a goose?

Author: Unknown

This fall when you see geese heading south for the winter, flying along in a "V" formation, you might be interested in knowing what science has discovered—why they fly in that formation. It was learned as each bird flaps its wings it creates uplift for the bird immediately following. By flying in a "V" formation the whole flock adds at least 75% greater flying range than if each bird flew on his own.

Basic Truth # 1:
People who share a common direction in a sense of community move quickly and easily because they are travelling on the thrust of one another.

Whenever a goose falls out of formation it suddenly feels the dragging resistance of going it alone and quickly gets back into the formation to take advantage of the lifting power of the bird immediately out in front.

Basic Truth # 2:

If we have as much sense as a goose we will stay in formation with those who are headed the same way we are going.

When the lead goose gets tired she rotates back into formation and another goose flies point.

Basic Truth # 3:

It pays to take turns doing hard jobs, with people or with geese flying south.

The geese honk from behind to encourage the ones up in the front to keep up their speed.

Basis Final Truth # 4:

We need to be careful what we say when we honk from behind.

Finally, when a goose gets sick or is wounded by gun shot and falls out, two geese fall out with it and follow it down to help it and protect it. They stay with it until it is either able to fly or until it is dead.

Then, they launch out on their own or with another formation to catch up with their own group.

The final truth:

If we have the sense of a goose we will stand by each other.

Mequietch,

Elder Stanley Stephens: End Note:

1. Indian Agent was the title of a position mandated by the
   Indian Act. Indian Agents held control over the lives of
   all Indian people in their jurisdictional area.

Part Four

Engaging the past . . .

Indian Residential Schools were the focus of an era in Canadian history that was dark for Aboriginal people. About 150,000 First Nations, Inuit and Métis children were taken from their families to attend the schools from as early as the 19th century to 1996. Missionaries ran most of the schools from the Roman Catholic, Anglican, Presbyterian and United churches.

Children were separated from their families and culture to be educated in a schooling system designed to crush their language and customs. For over one hundred and forty years, this shortsighted societal abuse of human rights, those of the "Indian," was a major part of a policy of forced integration.

In the 1990s the government of Canada and their Indian residential school church partners began a process to accept responsibility for the sins of their forefathers. Apologies were made with provision for financial resources being awarded to residential school survivors based on the number of years of attendance. Formal admission of past wrongs also opened pathways of cooperation whereby First Nations and the Government of Canada would work together in a trust relationship to find First Nation solutions to social and economic problems. No longer wards of the state, First Nations are to establish distinct partnership relationships within Canada's multicultural society.

Residential schools were established to assimilate Aboriginals into European-influenced Canadian society. Mandatory attendance in these government-funded boarding schools was seen as essential to the assimilation process. The important part was the removal of the children from their First Nation communities. The Government of Canada operated nearly every school as a joint venture with the Roman Catholic, Anglican, Methodist, United, or Presbyterian Church. There were approximately 130 residential schools in the territories and provinces across Canada.

Esther, Bunnie, and Stanley have told of their experiences. Thousands of children who attended the now infamous church-run Indian Residential Schools tell a similar story. It is important to note that Bunnie's experience was nowhere as challenging as Esther's and that of other children. Nonetheless their treatment, the forcible removable of children from their parents, and the separation from customs and traditions of their heritage, had the same effect. The children were alienated from their families and from a lifestyle in which they, and generations before them, had prospered despite the difficulties of life in the bush and the absence of the material goods of white "civilization."

For generations, Canada's First Nations people struggled to retain their identity and dignity. Aboriginal peoples now have First Nation status within the country that once went to great ends to destroy their very identity. But the abuse and alienation of past generations have left present generations victims of the shame and loneliness of their parents and grandparents who suffered the residential school experience.

With the resolve not to continue the draconian treatment of Canada's first people with its legacy of broken promises, and with the determination and vision of a better future, on January 7, 1998, Canada's Truth and Reconciliation Commission stated:

There is an emerging and compelling desire to put the events of the past behind us so that we can work towards a stronger and healthier future. The truth telling and reconciliation process as part of an overall holistic and comprehensive response to the Indian Residential School legacy is a sincere indication and acknowledgement of the injustices and harms experienced by Aboriginal people and the need for continued healing.

The reality is, though, that for Esther and others, no amount of money or sincere apologizing will ever mend the broken hearts and damaged spirit of people who endured the residential school experience. For her, the distance to a point where engrained prejudices and conceptions about native peoples and their approach to life are eliminated is still very far off in the future.

Others, like Stanley, had the lessons learned at school undermined and rendered useless because of the shame they experienced. Stanley became successful despite ill treatment but fully recognized that his generation and many others became unable to parent and set examples for their children, essential for culture and family.

Bunnie's realization that as an adult she wore a moccasin on one foot and a high-heeled shoe on the other is an insight into how we as individuals prosper and grow in a multicultural society.

We conclude here with the words of celebrated Elder and Hereditary Chief Robert Joseph's Honourary Doctorate of Law Acceptance Speech [1].

Chief Robert Joseph

Governor General Michaëlle Jean greets Chief
Robert Joseph

"What a great day this is,
what a special day!"

I would never have dreamed in a thousand years that I
could receive such an honour from this great institution,
University of British Columbia. There are no words to
describe this momentous occasion for me. I am deeply
moved to be so honoured and to share this stage with the
graduates before you.

I have long heard about the University of British Columbia and its tradition of excellence. I have known about others who have received honourary degrees here because of their distinction and stature. I used to think that such honour belonged only to the rich and famous, to the intelligentsia, to those born into the right circumstance, and to people of races other than my own.

It is with an even greater sense of humility that I accept this honourary degree. I would be remiss if I didn't thank Chancellor MacEachern, President Dr. Martha Piper, and the Senate of UBC. I also want to thank the selections committee and all of those people who formally supported my nomination. Thank you, Sharon Thira. Last but not least, thank you, family, friends, colleagues, and the community for giving inspiration to my life.

When I was six years old I ended up in an Indian residential school. I spent ten lost years of my life there. The only language I knew was Kwakwala. Almost from the very first day I entered that school I was beaten for speaking my birthright. I would cry myself to sleep at night, alone and terribly lonely. When I ran out of tears I would fantasize about being home with my family and being in my home community. There were many times that I was very hungry and sometimes the worms danced on top of my porridge.

There was so much pain, so much harm, and so much change in those 10 years at this school. And, there was much trauma. Sometimes the details are difficult to remember but you can never really forget.

I did not know then what the Royal Commission on Aboriginal People had since discovered, which was that the aim of Indian residential schooling was, "To kill the Indian in the child."

I did not realize that the goal of Sir John A. MacDonald and the federal government was "to eliminate Indians until there is not a single Indian left in Canada that has not been absorbed into the body politic."

I did not know that all Aboriginal people were undergoing a massive and traumatic alienation from their lands and cultures, families, and communities. Like thousands upon thousands of others, I left residential school a broken spirit. Without a spirit you have no spirituality. Without spirituality there is no hope, there is no peace.

Such is our shared legacy. For most Canadians this is Canada's secret. This university can and must help us to unlock this secret by educating all pupils to learn about this historic travesty.

I have travelled far and climbed many mountains in my life's journey. I have seen the darkness of my own abyss. From the depths of my utter despair and hopelessness I saw a miraculous vision. Through this vision I have seen the universe, one whole, one connectedness, one balance!

As I stood in awe of the wonder in my own supernatural moment, I came to know my place and part in this timeless symphony of life and creation. Before that, I was forced to relinquish my own reality for a while. I was taught to dismiss all that was prior to the coming of the first settlers. It was too high a price to exact for my education, for anyone's education.

I say to all you graduates beware that the price of your education does not become too high. Be true to yourselves. Maintain that balance between heart and soul and do not give away to intelligence only. Do not ever lose sight of who you are, for it is a gift from the creator that will lead you to your higher purpose. Do not give way to racism and intolerance. Do not give way to ignorance and apathy. Hold true to the creed that all persons are born equal and deserve dignity and respect. The quality of life for many may depend on you. Go and make a difference. The whole world waits for you.

In closing, I want to leave a few words with this great institution with so much tradition. Stay the course. Be bold. Have vision. Tell this country about the real history between us. Our mutual healing and reconciliation depend on it.

Many Aboriginals have passed through your doors—many more are coming. Encourage and support this trend. The House of Learning is a great place of transformation. Support it strongly.

See my vision; see the universe; see the whole; see the connectedness; see the balance.

We can no longer be apart—we must bring about balance and harmony. Let us belong to this time and place together."

"We must always remember that it is our mind, and that alone, that chains us or sets us free."
Gilakasla—Thank you.

Chief Robert Joseph,
Executive Director
Indian Residential School Survivor Society
British Columbia, Canada

Engaging the past: End Note:

1. On September 27, 2003, the University of British Columbia presented a honourary law degree to hereditary Chief Robert Joseph of the Kwagiulth nation of the northeast coast of Vancouver Island. Chief Joseph, the executive director of the Indian Residential School Survivors Society, has been involved in First Nations activities at the local, provincial, and national levels. Chief Joseph provided leadership, counselling, and support to former students of Indian residential schools and helped to improve relationships between Aboriginal and non-Aboriginal communities and governments.

Part Five

Introduction
To
Historical Background

Every person, place, thing, and happening has a history, but few make it into the history books. It has been said that: "History is little more than the crimes, follies and misfortunes of mankind[2]." Canada had for a long time omitted telling the history of the residential schools. We have a four-hundred-year story of Euro-Canadian and Indian relations that defies a single narrative and for this reason Part Five is a historic narrative of supporting histories pertaining to Indian residential schools. This has been done

---

[2]   Excerpted in part: Truth and Reconciliation Commission of Canada—www.trc-cvr.ca/about.html

so the reader can better know the people, the places, and the errors in the complex history behind the story.

There is a premise that the residential school program of forced assimilation was well intended. No such argument can be made for how the program was executed. The people in charge, the Government of Canada abandoned the principles of accountability to the most trusted of institutions, the churches, to deliver the program, thus absolving themselves of any responsibility.

Esther, Bunnie, and Stanley tell their stories as events that happened to them and their families. Thousands who attended the now infamous church-run institutions could tell the same story. Beginning in the 1870s, there came to be over 130 such schools located across Canada, and the last of them only closed in 1996. These schools were set up to eliminate parental involvement in the raising of their children. The intention was for the Aboriginal population to assimilate into European-influenced Canadian society. These were government-funded boarding schools, where Aboriginal children were sent to learn about European-Canadian Christian culture. The Government of Canada operated nearly every school as a joint venture with the Roman Catholic, Anglican, Methodist, United, or Presbyterian Church.

Beginning in the 1980s, with the support of the Assembly of First Nations and Inuit organizations, former residential school students took the federal government and the churches to court. Their cases led to the Indian Residential Schools Settlement Agreement, the largest class-action settlement of any kind in Canadian history. The agreement sought to begin repairing the harm caused by residential schools. Aside from providing compensation to former students, the agreement called for the establishment of the Truth and Reconciliation Commission of Canada with a budget of $60 million over five years.

On June 11, 2008, the Prime Minister, on behalf of the Government of Canada, delivered a formal apology in the House of Commons to former students, their families, and communities for Canada's role in the operation of the residential schools.

We cannot escape from history. Our lives are governed by what happened in the past our decisions by what we believe to have happened. Without knowledge of history, humankind and society would run adrift, paddling on the uncharted river of time. Learning about the past, and presenting it is important.

The 1996 report from the Royal Commission on Aboriginal Peoples made an interesting observation about Aboriginal and non-Aboriginal approaches to history:

Before 1500, Aboriginal societies in the Americas and non-Aboriginal societies in Europe developed along separate paths, in ignorance of one another. Rendering accurately the history of a cross-cultural relationship is not simple or straightforward. History is not an exact science. Past events have been recorded and interpreted by human beings who, much like ourselves, have understood them through the filter of their own values, perceptions and general philosophies of life and society. Important differences derive from the methodology of history—how the past is examined, recorded and communicated. The non-Aboriginal historical tradition in Canada is rooted in western scientific methodology and emphasized scholarly documentation and written records.

In the non-Aboriginal tradition, at least until recently, the purpose of historical study has often been the analysis of particular events in an effort to establish what "really" happened as a matter of objective historical truth or, more modestly, to marshal fact in support of a particular interpretation of past events. However, document analyses will never give you the full story. You also have to hear the personal story and song of those affected to understand the moral dimension of historical interpretations. This cuts across many of the other historical interpretations: how we in the present judge actors in different circumstances in the past; how different interpretations of the past reflect different moral stances today; when and how crimes of the past bear consequences today, such as what is to be done today, about the legacy of Indian Residential Schools? Taken together, these tie "historical thinking" to competencies in "Historical Literacy."

The Aboriginal tradition in the recording of history is neither linear nor steeped in the same notions of social progress and evolution. Nor is it usual only human-centered in the same way as the western scientific tradition, for it does not assume that human beings are anything more than one—and not necessarily the most important—element of the natural order of the universe. Moreover, the Aboriginal historical tradition is an oral one, involving legends, stories and accounts handed down through the generations in oral form. It is less focused on establishing objective truth and assumes that the teller of the story is so much a part of the event being described that it would be arrogant to presume precise accuracy and time.

Unlike western scientific tradition, which creates a sense of distance in time between the listener or reader and the events being described, the tendency of Aboriginal perspectives is to create a sense of immediacy by encouraging listeners to imagine they are participating in the past being recounted.

For this reason imagine that you are there, as we tell of the linear history of European arrival to the new world, the fur trade, the Christianization of natives, the colonization, and the subsequent policies and actions that were to the disadvantage of Canada's original inhabitants. Most of all, envision yourself being taken from your parents and placed in a residential school at the age of seven or younger.

Wemistikoskiw (White-Men)

Knives, Iron Cooking Pots, Guns, Traps, Beads and Blankets

When Europeans discovered Hudson Bay and James Bay, they found tundra in the north, and in the south, a mix of jack pine, tamarack, balsam fir, and balsam poplar trees that teemed with fur-bearing animals of many kinds. The Cree, as well as most Aboriginal people living in the "New World" hunted these animals for food and for their skins to dress themselves. A favourite clothing material was the beautiful inner wool-like fur of the beaver pelt. The early arriving French and English eventually realized that it was not Cathay's gold but the pelts of the beaver that were the treasure. They soon began trading with the native people for their furs and the "Indians" were quick to discover the appeal of iron cooking pots, knives, blankets and guns, as well as traps to catch more fur. Thus began "The Fur Trade."

In 1670, King Charles II made the Company of Adventurers of England trading into Hudson Bay, "the true and absolute Lordes and Proprietors of Rupert's Land."

The Hudson's Bay Company was granted "sole trade and commerce" in fur in the vast drainage area of the Hudson and James Bay regions of what is now Canada.

A successful fur trade could only be established if the fur industry in Europe could create a demand for fur-trimmed clothing . . . this came through as a new fashion in men's hats. Large, felt beaver fur hats became the craze and thus the great demand for beaver pelts brought about the fur trade in North America. This brought on struggles with the French, who challenged the English entry into the American fur trade of the north.

Much has been written about the history of the Hudson's Bay Company, its rivals and conflicts. Less reported was the rough life of its people in the early days of the fur trade and in particular the rough life of the people manning their fur trading posts in the Canadian north. More often than not, the workers recruited by the Company were among the poor of England and Scotland who arrived with their usual bronchial troubles and other ailments rendering them unprepared to face a life of hardship in a northern climate. The traders who came in search of the pelts of fur-bearing animals were not northerners and knew little about how to survive a Canadian winter. At first they did not make an effort to learn from the Cree and Inuit about how to survive in this rigorous climate. They knew nothing about the animals; little to nothing about the people of the region, and that life in the north does not necessarily need be one of hardship.

Imagine working outdoors at the edge of the Arctic Ocean, where stoves and open fires did little to warm unsuited European-style buildings. The extreme winter cold caused severe frostbite and snow blindness, and in the summer there were the inescapable mosquitoes and black flies. It was a life of hardship and horror for the new arrivals until they adapted basic Inuit and Cree architectural principles that enable a small space to be heated comfortably with small fires and blubber-fueled lamps. The Cree, like other first nations people, had survived this harsh and unforgiving climate for many centuries before the arrival of the Europeans.

The Hudson's Bay Company established Moose Factory on Hudson Bay and Fort Albany on James Bay and smaller trading posts inland to trade for fur harvested mostly by native trappers. Native communities were, or became, established at trading post locations. There was not only competition between fur-trading companies for furs but also between the Anglican and Roman Catholic Churches to Christianize native people.

For many decades, Aboriginals were commercial partners and allies of the arriving Europeans, but after the War of 1812 when the Europeans had settled their quarrels about who ruled or owned North American, Canadian society decided that "Indians" were an irrelevant nuisance. This was the century in which Aboriginal people throughout Canada declined in great numbers. The decline was the direct consequence of government and church policies adopted towards them and the attempt to develop a European civilization in the new land. With the arrival of more Europeans came the introduction and the spread of diseases, such as smallpox, for which the native population had no natural immunity.

An effort to reduce conflict between development and First Nations' loss of territory brought measures that threatened to undermine the base of Aboriginal identity and the survival of their territories.

One dreadful policy was piled on another, year after year. The policies of enfranchisement (the Crown assuming absolute power and authority), of forcing "Indians" to abandon their status and identity, of setting aside the Royal Proclamation provisions regarding Indian lands, of enforced education in residential schools, and the surrender treaties, removing Indians from the path of development all had their origin in the decades before Confederation.

A century and a half of attempts by Euro-Canadian society to define the role of natives and to impose that destiny failed. Aside from the effective removal of Indians from the land, none of the policies have been successful. Attempts by governments, churches and the general population to change Indians, Métis and Inuit into just another ethnic group in the multicultural mosaic have failed.[3]

What history often fails to comment on were the sacrifices made by Aboriginal people:

- Change from a traditional hunter-gatherer lifestyle to one of commercial fur-trappers.

- Giving up their "hard to pronounce" names through relationships, or more often by being told that your name is now Stevens or some other Scottish or English surname.

- Being pushed off their traditional hunting and trapping territory in favour of white trappers and settlers.

- The dreadful impact of the introduction of alcohol.

The lives of native people were profoundly changed by the arrival of the Europeans, as their daily lives changed, they found that they had to develop new ways to survive, such as participating in mutually beneficial trading arrangements with the Europeans, who typically misunderstood native ways.

---

[3] /16 Professor J. R. Miller of the University of Toronto, in his book, Skyscrapers Hide the Heavens: A History of Indian-White Relations in Canada, (1989).

From the many interviews the author had with Esther, Bunnie, and Stanley, it became clear that they were not concerned with the many and the various points-of-view: they were concerned with the truth. Facts are selected and others are ignored. Facts can mislead and they sometimes do, and they may also be self-serving. Said another way, history is biased by whoever tells the story. Esther, Bunnie, and Stanley believe strongly that it is their responsibility to tell their story in order to create a better future. Evidence is taken from the spoken word of people who have knowledge of past events and traditions. This oral history is often recorded and put in writing. It is used in history books and to document land claims.

What conventional history has failed to fully mention is the debate whether to assimilate the "Indians" or simply to let the carnage of smallpox and starvation prevail—leaving their fate in the hands of God.

Canada's policy of forced assimilation and the Indian residential schools was an attempt to destroy Aboriginal culture. This prevailed for seven generations. Note: During the early days of Confederation there were many negotiations and treaty signings. Through treaties, native sovereignty over land was relinquished for government promises of economic assistance, educational facilities, and the creation of reserves. The Royal Canadian Mounted Police presence was a visible manifestation of power and authority representative of the larger Canadian society, its institutions, customs, and laws.

Esther asks, "Bob, why did they do this to me?"

To answer Esther's often-asked question, "Why did they do this to me?" we must look at Canada's early relationship with First Nations. The English and French crowns, both anxious to attain glory and wealth through exploration and conquest in what is now Eastern Canada, named and befriended the Aboriginal people. They called them "Indians" because, not knowing the size of the world, they believed upon first arriving in the New World that they had reached India. Awed by advanced technology and trade, the "Indians" became allies for and against the English and French, who competed for supremacy. However the "Indians" were unaware that the English and French were fighting for supremacy over their own First Nation territories.

When the British Empire's claim for Canada was confirmed and there was no longer a threat of territorial acquisition by the United States after the War of 1812, the Indian was deemed to be a problem to be managed. The Crown could not have self-reliant free-roaming

Aboriginals with no cultural concept of land ownership becoming surly and hostile over the loss of their territory. If this were permitted, it would have obstructed European land settlement in Upper Canada. It was also of concern to the Crown that the Aboriginal lifestyle was becoming increasingly difficult to maintain as wildlife was becoming more scarce. The time had come to change the rules.

The "Indian situation" had to be managed so the Crown deemed itself trustee for management of the Aboriginals. To that end, in 1830 Sir George Murray[4] on behalf of the British Imperial government announced a radical change in the long-standing policy pertaining to the Indians of Upper and Lower Canada. He said that time for friendship with the First Nations had passed now that the war with the United States was over. He went on to say that it was now in the Crown's best interest for the purpose of governing, the management of agriculture, and the expanding European settlements, to impose upon the Aboriginals the industrious and peaceful habits of civilized life.

The Indian Act, first passed by Canada in 1876 and revised in 1880, imposed Federal Government control over, virtually all aspects of Aboriginal daily life. The Indian Act established the Crown as responsible for educating and caring for the country's Aboriginal people. It focused

---

[4]   Sir George Murray (1772-1864)

on three main areas: band councils, reserves, and status (membership). The primary purpose was (and still is) to control natives and assimilate them into Canadian society. It was always intended as a temporary set of laws until native peoples were successfully assimilated. The government thought that the "Indians" best chance for success was for them to learn to speak English and adopt Christianity and European-Canadian customs and values. The thinking of the day was that Indian children would then pass on their adopted lifestyle to their children, and that native traditions would diminish, or be completely eliminated in a matter of a few generations.

The Indian Act defined Aboriginal people by creating for them a separate identity, making them wards of the state. It also banned Aboriginal ceremonies and made separate provisions for men and women. For example, if an Indian woman married a white man, she and their children lost their rights under the Indian Act. If an Indian man married a white woman she and their children were given the same rights that her husband had under the Indian Act. The Indian Act is a legal statute of laws passed by the Parliament of Canada that has also been changed by successive Parliaments. The Indian Act of 1927 prohibited Indians from hiring lawyers, and Indian war veterans were not accorded the same compensation as non-native veterans. It was not until 1960 that Indians received the right to vote in Canadian elections.

The federal policy of assimilation had its origin in the Gradual Civilization Act of 1857 that was reinforced by the Indian Act of 1876 and sanctioned by successive parliaments of Canada. The policy was one of "aggressive assimilation," whereby Indian youth were to be taught at church-run, government-funded industrial schools, later called Indian residential schools or industrial schools.

Timeline of forced integration:

- The first official law was passed in 1857 to replace indigenous culture with European culture in the Canadian Legislative Assembly and Council. The act was "to Encourage Gradual Civilization of Indian Tribes of this Province."

- At confederation on July 1, 1867, Canada was declared a sovereign nation. All provinces were recognized and powers were divided between the Federal Government and the Provinces. The federal government assumed responsibility over Aboriginals and the lands that were to be reserved for them.

- The Department of Indian Affairs was directed to better the conditions of Aboriginal communities by encouraging them, in every possible manner, in the acquisition of religious knowledge and practical education.

- The government developed a "Policy of Civilization" that was to become the foundation for the creation of Indian Reserves. Areas of Crown Land, as determined by the Department of Indian Affairs, were set aside for the exclusive use of First Nation people.

- Treaties were signed with the Indians, who assumed that they retained their full Aboriginal rights, not having been informed of the limitations of the Indian Act.

- The Indian Act was drafted from the consolidation of several pieces of discriminatory legislation, including the section that resulted in Indian women losing their Indian status and membership when they married non-status men.

- The first residential schools built by the government and run by the churches opened in 1883.

- In 1920, education became mandatory for Aboriginal children, and, where necessary they were forcibly taken from their families by clergy, Indian agents, and law enforcement officers.

- By 1931, 80 residential schools were operating in Canada.

- During the 1950s, residential schools began to close their doors.

  o 1951 changes to the Indian Act gave provinces the authority to create their own laws and policies where federal authority did not exist.

  o Provinces implemented laws making it possible for them to take Aboriginal children into their care.

- During the 1960s—"The 60s Scoop" thousands of Aboriginal children were taken from their families by the provinces. They were placed into foster care, adopted, or institutionalized with no hope of returning home.

- Child and Family Caring Society reported that many Aboriginal children were taken into custody due to issues of poverty and neglect rather than maltreatment, which is in contrast to non-Aboriginal people's experience.

o More children were then in foster care than at the height of the residential schools.

o Hard-to-place and problem children were systematically placed in varying levels of detention or treatment centres.

• By 1979, only 12 residential schools remained, with 1,899 students.

• In the 1980s, former residential school students begin to tell of sexual and other forms of abuse they had received at school.

• A 1985 Act to Amend the Indian Act eliminated the gender discrimination, and enabled people affected by the discriminatory provisions of the old Indian Act to have their Indian status and membership restored.

• In 1996 Akaitcho Hall in Yellowknife became the last residential school to close.

- In 1998 the Aboriginal Healing Foundation was established to aid the 150,000 survivors of Indian Residential Schools, their families and communities.

- In 2007 the federal government offered residential school survivors a total of $1.9 billion in compensation for the abuse they suffered in residential schools.

- The federal government, and the major church partners, except the Roman Catholic Church, gave formally apologies to the residential school survivors for their role and the abuse of students. The Roman Catholic Church has never "apologized" merely offered an "expression of sorrow."

- In 2008 Prime Minister Stephen Harper gave a formal apology to residential school survivors for the government's role in financing residential schools.

- By 2008, $1.19 billion in federal compensation had been paid out to 61,473 residential school survivors.

Although Esther's ancestors, the Cree people of western James Bay, were not uncooperative, and their traditional territory was not needed for development, they came under the same government domination as all Aboriginals in

Canada. The Indian residential schools program, intended, in the words of an 1870 government official, "to bring these children into the circle of civilization," was a problem fraught with difficulty from the time of its inception. The government-church partners were not only aware of the sorrowful circumstances of the schools but also claimed otherwise. In 1939, an illustrated pamphlet of the Anglican Church asked parishioners to sponsor individual children in their care. In this pamphlet, well-dressed and happy children were shown learning and benefitting from academic and industrial skills taught to them at the schools. Children were shown sitting nicely at tables eating tasty, and nourishing-looking meals of milk, vegetables and fresh meat, food proudly produced by the children for themselves thanks to the schools' industrial training program. In reality, the schools were badly underfunded and in 1938 the Department of Indian Affairs funded the churches managing the Indian Residential Schools with an annual payment of, $180 per student. In relative terms of today's money, $180 would equate to about $3,600. To some this may seem like a lot but it was way below what was needed, by comparison, to keep a person in a minimum security prison—which is not all that dissimilar to an Indian residential school.

Canada was not alone in these actions. Following an Australian government edict in 1931, Aboriginal children and children of mixed marriages were gathered up by the whites and taken to settlements to be assimilated. At the settlements children were forbidden to speak their native language, forced to abandon their Aboriginal heritage, and taught to be culturally white. The United States had similar programs; throughout the country children were taken from Indian Reservations and put into Indian Schools far from their homes.

In 1948, the United Nations convened a meeting on the prevention and punishment of the crime of genocide that defined it to include the following acts committed with the intent to destroy, in whole or in part, a national, ethnic, racial or religious group:

a. Killing members of the group.
b. Causing serious bodily or mental harm to members of the group.
c. Deliberately inflicting on the group conditions of life calculated to bring about its physical destruction in whole or in part.
d. Imposing measures intended to prevent birth within the group.
e. Forcibly transferring children of the group to another group.

Prior to the 1960s, the federal government gave little consideration to the value of native culture and values. This changed as considerable political pressure was brought to bear by First Nations calling for more control over their own affairs.

The residential school program did not achieve its aims, but it did cause suffering, humiliation and marginalization for generations of Canadian Aboriginal people. Thousands of First Nations People across Canada and are compromised as a result of the Indian Act.

Each of these interrelated social injustices required a unique and complicated fix. The saying, "For every complicated problem there is a simple solution but it is usually wrong," has never been truer. A simple solution for Indian Residential Schools would have been to just close them. Not so fast! The program was seen by policy makers in Ottawa in the 1940s to be a failure but it took until 1996 for the last residential school in Canada to close its doors. Why?

First, some church administrations, as well some First Nation communities, opposed the closing of these facilities. The primary educational role of many of the schools had shifted to one of social services for native children requiring foster homes. There were an ever-increasing number of parents unable to care for their children because of alcoholism, poor parenting skills, and home circumstances. There were also serious cultural issues with Aboriginal and non-Aboriginal integrated schooling. Integrated educational environments were seen as hostile to native children and the schools were not well equipped, sufficiently staffed, or understanding of the needs of native children. There were jurisdictional issues between the provinces, Department of Indian Affairs, and First Nations. The residential schools were still perceived as positive efforts. The government and churches alike did not begin to fully address their responsibilities until the 1990s.

In 1990, Chief Phil Fontaine and the Assembly of First Nations called for the churches involved to acknowledge the physical, emotional, and sexual abuse endured by residential school students. Chief Fontaine, himself a former residential school attendee, presented a clear and forceful message, "We cannot change the fact that a great social injustice did occur but the time is long overdue for us to acknowledge that it did happen and it was wrong."

Since the late 1990s, former Indian Residential School students pressed, often through litigation, for acknowledgment of and compensation for suffering and abuse. Native communities, with some churches supporting, and government financial assistance since 1998, established support programs for people with residual issues resulting from family breakdown, violence, and the aimlessness brought about by residential schools.

In 2006, the government of Canada convened a Royal Commission on Aboriginal People, and a year later, in 2007 formalized a $1.9 billion compensation package for those people who were forced to attend Indian Residential Schools funded under the Indian Act by Indian and Northern Affairs Canada. These schools were run by churches of various denominations—about sixty per cent by Roman Catholics and thirty per cent by the Anglican Church of Canada and the United Church of Canada, along with its pre-1925 predecessors, the Presbyterian, Congregationalist, and Methodist churches. The Federal Government provided facilities and maintenance and the churches provided teachers and education.

A settlement agreement reached in May 2006 provided funding for an Aboriginal Healing Foundation program in Aboriginal communities, and a Common Experience Payment to those who had attended Indian Residential Schools. The amount of compensation was based on the number of years a particular former student resided in the residential schools: $10,000 for the first year attended plus $3,000 for every year attended thereafter. In addition to financial compensation, the responsible parties made apologies.

Common Experience Payments (CEP) became available to all the former students of residential schools on September 19, 2007. Former students who met certain criteria had to apply to receive their full compensation. The deadline to apply for the CEP was September 19, 2011. Additional compensation became available to individuals who experienced excessive abuse and/or sexual assault. An application deadline of September 19, 2012, was set for an Independent Assessment Process.

The Independent Assessment Process (IAP) is supposed to be a claimant-centred, non-adversarial, out-of-court process for the resolution of claims of sexual abuse, serious physical abuse, and other wrongful acts suffered.

Appendix I

List of the Indian Residential Schools[5]

British Columbia

- Alberni Indian Residential School (PB)
- Ahousaht Indian Residential School (PB)
- Christie Indian Residential School (RC)
- Cowichan Catholic Convent School (RC)
- Friendly Cove Day School (MD)
- Kamloops Indian Residential School (RC)
- Kitimat Indian Residential School (MD)
- Kootenay Indian Residential School (RC)
- Kuper Island Indian Residential School (RC)
- Lejac Residential School (RC)
- Lower Post Indian Residential School (RC)
- Methodist Coqualeetza Institute (MD)

---

5 Wikipedia Free Encyclopedia

- Metlakatla Indian Residential School (OO)
- Port Simpson Methodist Girl's School (MD)
- Presbyterian Coqualeetza Indian Residential School (PB)
- Roman Catholic Coqualeetza Indian Residential School (RC)
- Sechelt Indian Residential School (RC)
- Squamish Indian Residential School (RC)
- St. George's Indian Residential School (AN)
- St. Mary's Mission Indian Residential School (RC)
- St. Michael's Indian Residential School (AN)
- Thomas Crosby Indian Residential School (MD)
- Victoria Catholic Convent School (RC)
- Williams Lake Indian Residential School (RC)
- Yale Indian Residential School (AN)
- Yuquot Indian Residential School (RC)

Alberta

- Assumption Indian Residential School (RC)
- Blue Quill's Indian Residential School (RC)
- Convent of Holy Angels Indian Residential School (RC)
- Crowfoot Indian Residential School (RC)
- Dunbow Industrial School (RC)
- Edmonton Industrial School (MD)
- Ermineskin Indian Residential School (RC)

- Fort Smith Indian Residential School RC)
- Immaculate Conception Indian Residential School (RC)
- Immaculate Conception Boarding School (RC)
- McDougall Orphanage and Residential School (MD)
- Old Sun's Boarding School (AN)
- Old Sun's Boarding School (North Camp School (AN)
- Peigan Indian Residential School (AN)
- Red Deer Industrial School (MD)
- Sarcee Indian Residential School (AN)
- St. Albert's Indian Residential School (RC)
- St. Andrew's Indian Residential School (AN)
- St. Barnabas Indian Residential School (AN)
- St. Bernard Indian Residential School (RC)
- St. Bruno Indian Residential School (RC)
- St. Cyprian's Indian Residential School (AN)
- St. Francis Xavier Indian Residential School (RC)
- St. Henri Indian Residential School (RC)
- St. John's Indian Residential School (AN)
- St. Martin Boarding School (RC)
- St. Paul Des Métis Indian Residential School (RC)
- St. Paul's Indian Residential School (AN)
- St. Peter's Indian Residential School (AN)
- Sturgeon Lake Indian Residential School (RC)
- Youville Indian Residential School (RC)

Saskatchewan

- Battleford Industrial School (RC)
- Beauval Indian Residential School (RC) (became Meadow Lake Tribal Council's Beauval Indian Educational Centre)
- Cowesses Indian Residential School (RC)
- Crowstand Indian Residential School (PB)
- St. Michael's Indian Residential School (RC)
- Emmanuel College (AN)
- File Hills Indian Residential School (MD)
- Gordon Indian Residential School (AN)
- Guy Hill Indian Residential School (RC)
- Île-à-la-Crosse Indian Residential School (RC)
- Lake La Ronge Mission Indian Residential School (AN)
- Muscowequan Indian Residential School (RC)
- Prince Albert Indian Residential School (AN)
- Qu'Appelle Indian Residential School (RC)
- Regina Indian Residential School (PB)
- Round Lake Indian Residential School (MD)
- St. Anthony's Indian Residential School (RC)
- St. Barnabas Indian Residential School (AN)
- St. Phillips Indian Residential School (RC)
- Thunderchild Indian Residential School (RC)

Manitoba

- Assiniboia Indian Residential School (RC)
- Birtle Indian Residential School (PB)
- Brandon Indian Residential School (MD)
- Cross Lake Indian Residential School (RC)
- Elkhorn Indian Residential School (AN)
- Fort Alexander Indian Residential School RC)
- Guy Hill Indian Residential School (RC)
- Lake St. Martin Indian Residential School (AN)
- MacKay Indian Residential School (AN)
- Norway House Methodist Indian Residential School (MD)
- Pine Creek Indian Residential School (RC)
- Portage la Prairie Methodist Indian Residential School (MD)
- Portage la Prairie Presbyterian Indian Residential (PB)
- Sandy Bay Indian Residential School (RC)
- St. Boniface Industrial School RC)
- St. Paul's Industrial School (AN)
- Waterhen Indian Residential School (RC)

Ontario

- Albany Mission Indian Residential School (RC)
- Alexandra Industrial School for Girls (OO)
- Alnwick Industrial School (MD)
- Bishop Horden Memorial School (AN)

- Cecilia Jeffrey Indian Residential School (PB)
- Chapleau Indian Residential School (AN)
- Fort Frances Indian Residential School (RC)
- Kenora Indian Residential School (RC)
- McIntosh Indian Residential School; opened 1924; closed 1969 (RC)
- Mohawk Institute Residential School (AN)
- Mount Elgin Indian Residential School (MD)
- Shingwauk Indian Residential School (AN)
- Pelican Lake Indian Residential School (AN)
- Spanish Indian Residential School (RC)
- St. Anne's Indian Residential School (RC)
- St. Joseph's Indian Boarding School (RC)
- St. Mary's Indian Residential School (RC)
- Wikwemikong Indian Residential School (RC)
- Armstrong Indian Residential School (RC)
- Crystal Lake
- Stirlan Lake

Quebec

- Amos Indian Residential School (RC)
- Federal Hostel at George River
- Federal Hostel at Great Whale River
- Federal Hostel at Payne Bay
- Federal Hostel at Port Harrison

- Fort George Hostels
- Fort George (AN)
- Fort George (RC)
- La Tuque Indian Residential School (AN)
- Pointe Bleue Indian Residential School (RC)

Nova Scotia
- Shubenacadie Indian Residential School (RC)

Yukon
- Aklavik Anglican Indian Residential School (AN)
- Baptist Indian Residential School (BP)
- Carcross Indian Residential School (AN)
- St. Paul's Indian Residential School (AN)
- Yukon Hall; Whitehorse (AN)

Northwest Territories
- Aklavik Anglican Indian Residential School (AN)
- Aklavik Catholic Indian Residential School (RC)
- Fort McPherson Indian Residential School (OO)
- Fort Providence Indian Residential School (RC)
- Fort Resolution Indian Residential School (RC)
- Fort Simpson Indian Residential School (RC)
- Fort Simpson Indian Residential School (OO)
- Hay River Indian Residential School (AN)
- Yellowknife Indian Residential School (RC)

Nunavut

- Chesterfield Inlet Indian Residential School (RC)
- Frobisher Bay Indian Residential School (RC)

Religious Denominations:

(AN)   Anglican Church of Canada

(BP)   Baptist

(MD)   Methodist

(OO)   Other

(PB)   Presbyterian

(RC)   Roman Catholic

(UC)   United Church of Canada

Appendix II

Indian Residential School Apologies

2008—The Government of Canada Prime Minister Stephen Harper:[6]

I stand before the House of Parliament today to offer an apology to former students of Indian residential schools. The treatment of children in Indian residential schools is a sad chapter in our history.

In the 1870s, the federal government, partly in order to meet its obligation to educate Aboriginal children, began to play a role in the development and administration of these schools. Two primary objectives of the residential schools system were to remove and isolate children from the

---

[6]   http://www.cbc.ca/news/canada/story/2008/06/11/pm-statement.html

influence of their homes, families, traditions and cultures, and to assimilate them into the dominant culture.

These objectives were based on the assumption Aboriginal cultures and spiritual beliefs were inferior and unequal. Indeed, some sought, as it was infamously said, "to kill the Indian in the child." Today, we recognize that this policy of assimilation was wrong, has caused great harm, and has no place in our country. Most schools were operated as joint ventures with Anglican, Catholic, Presbyterian or United churches.

The Government of Canada built an educational system in which very young children were often forcibly removed from their homes, often taken far from their communities. Many were inadequately fed, clothed and housed. All were deprived of the care and nurturing of their parents, grandparents and communities. First Nations, Inuit and Metis languages and cultural practices were prohibited in these schools. Tragically, some of these children died while attending residential schools and others never returned home.

The government now recognizes that the consequences of the Indian residential schools' policy were profoundly negative and that this policy has had a lasting and damaging impact on Aboriginal culture, heritage and language.

While some former students have spoken positively about their experiences at residential schools these stories are far overshadowed by tragic accounts of the emotional, physical and sexual abuse and neglect of helpless children and their separation from powerless families and communities.

The legacy of Indian residential schools has contributed to social problems that continue to exist in many communities today. It has taken extraordinary courage for the thousands of survivors that have come forward to speak publicly about the abuse they suffered. It is a testament to their resilience as individuals and to the strength of their cultures. Regrettably, many former students are not with us today and died never having received a full apology from the government of Canada.

The government recognizes that the absence of an apology has been an impediment to healing and reconciliation. Therefore, on behalf of the government of Canada and all Canadians, I stand before you, in this chamber as central to our life as a country, to apologize to Aboriginal peoples for Canada's role in the Indian residential schools system. To the approximately 80,000 living former students, and all family members and communities, the government of Canada now recognizes that it was wrong to forcibly remove children from their homes and we apologize for having done this.

We now recognize that, in separating children from their families, we undermined the ability of many to adequately parent their own children and sowed the seeds for generations to follow and we apologize for having done this. We now recognize that, far too often, these institutions gave rise to abuse or neglect and were inadequately controlled, and we apologize for failing to protect you. Not only did you suffer these abuses as children but also as you became parents, you were powerless to protect your own children from suffering the same experience, and for this we are sorry.

The burden of this experience has been on your shoulders for far too long. The burden is properly ours as a government, and as a country. There is no place in Canada for the attitudes that inspired the Indian residential schools system to ever again prevail.

You have been working on recovering from this experience for a long time and in a very real sense, we are now joining you on this journey. The government of Canada sincerely apologizes and asks the forgiveness of the Aboriginal peoples of this country for failing them so profoundly. We are sorry.

In moving towards healing, reconciliation and resolution of the sad legacy of Indian residential schools, implementation of the Indian residential schools settlement agreement began on September 19, 2007. Years of work by survivors, communities, and Aboriginal organizations culminated in an agreement that gives us a new beginning and an opportunity to move forward together in partnership.

A cornerstone of the settlement agreement is the Indian Residential Schools Truth and Reconciliation Commission. This commission presents a unique opportunity to educate all Canadians on the Indian residential schools system.

It will be a positive step in forging a new relationship between Aboriginal peoples and other Canadians, a relationship based on the knowledge of our shared history, a respect for each other and a desire to move forward together with a renewed understanding that strong families, strong communities and vibrant cultures and traditions will contribute to a stronger Canada for all of us. God bless all of you and God bless our land.

Robert P. Wells

1993—Anglican Church of Canada[7]

Archbishop Michael Peers—To the National Native Convocation:[8]

My Brothers and Sisters: Together here with you I have listened as you have told your stories of the residential schools. I have heard the voices that have spoken of pain and hurt experienced in the schools, and of the scars, which endure to this day. I have felt shame and humiliation as I have heard of suffering inflicted by my people, and as I think of the part our church played in that suffering. I am deeply conscious of the sacredness of the stories that you have told and I hold in the highest honour those who have told them.

I have heard with admiration the stories of people and communities who have worked at healing, and I am aware of how much healing is needed. I also know that I am in need of healing, and my own people are in need of healing, and our church is in need of healing. Without that healing, we will continue the same attitudes that have done such damage in the past. I also know that healing takes a long

---

[7] In 1955, the church changed its name from "the Church of England in the Dominion of Canada" to "the Anglican Church of Canada.

[8] http://www.anglican.ca/relationships/trc/apology/english

time, both for people and for communities. I also know that it is God who heals, and that God can begin to heal when we open ourselves our wounds, our failures, and our shame to God. I want to take one step along that path here and now. I accept and I confess before God and you, our failures in the residential schools. We failed you. We failed ourselves. We failed God.

I am sorry, more than I can say, that we were part of a system, which took you and your children from home and family. I am sorry, more than I can say, that we tried to remake you in our image, taking from you your language and the signs of your identity. I am sorry, more than I can say, that in our schools so many were abused physically, sexually, culturally, and emotionally. On behalf of the Anglican Church of Canada, I present our apology. I do this at the desire of those in the Church like the National Executive Council, who know some of your stories and have asked me to apologize.

I do this in the name of many who do not know these stories. And I do this even though there are those in the church who cannot accept the fact that these things were done in our name. As soon as I am home, I shall tell all the bishops what I have said, and ask them to co-operate with me and with the National Executive Council in helping this healing at the local level. Some bishops have already begun this work. I know how often you have heard words, which have been empty because they have not been accompanied by actions. I pledge to you my best efforts, and the efforts of our church at the national level, to walk with you along the path of God's healing.

The work of the Residential Schools Working Group, the video, the commitment and the effort of the Special Assistants to the Primate for this work, the grants available for healing conferences, are some signs of that pledge, and we shall work for others. This is Friday, the day of Jesus' suffering and death. It is the anniversary of the first atomic bomb at Hiroshima, one of the most terrible injuries ever inflicted by one people on another. But even atomic bombs and Good Friday are not the last word. God raised Jesus from the dead as a sign that life and wholeness are the everlasting and unquenchable purpose of God. Thank you for listening to me.

2009—The Roman Catholic Church[9]

The Roman Catholic Church did approximately 70% of the forced Indian Residential Schooling in Canada. Pope Benedict expressed his sorrow for the suffering of Aboriginal people in Canada's residential schools to the Assembly of First Nations' National Chief, Phil Fontaine, in April of 2009. However, the Roman Catholic Church refuses to formally apologize for its role in Canada's policy of forced Aboriginal assimilation and Indian Residential Schooling. At the centre of this refusal to apologize lies the irrevocable papal bull *Romanus Pontifex* issued in 1455 by Pope Nicholas V. Centuries of destruction and genocide resulted from the application of this document and its framework of dominance against Indigenous Peoples and their lands, territories and resources.

Chief Fontaine had a meeting, funded by Indian and Northern Affairs Canada, with Pope Benedict XVI to try to obtain an apology for abuses that occurred in the residential school system. Following the meeting, the Vatican released an official statement on the church's role in residential schools:

His Holiness recalled that since the earliest days of her presence in Canada, the Church, particularly through

---

9   http://caid.ca/church_apology.htm

her missionary personnel, has closely accompanied the indigenous peoples. Given the sufferings that some indigenous children experienced in the Canadian Residential School system, the Holy Father expressed his sorrow at the anguish caused by the deplorable conduct of some members of the Church and he offered his sympathy and prayerful solidarity. His Holiness emphasized that acts of abuse cannot be tolerated in society. He prayed that all those affected would experience healing, and he encouraged First Nations Peoples to continue to move forward with renewed hope.

Fontaine later stated at a news conference that at the meeting, he sensed the Pope's "pain and anguish" and that the acknowledgement was "important" to him and that was what he was looking for.

The Catholic Church has never officially apologized for any abuse. Yes, they have "expressed sorrow," and yes, for whatever political or other reason, Chief Fontaine\claimed to be happy with that—but the Catholic Church has never apologized.

1994—Presbyterian Church of Canada[10]

Our Confession

The Holy Spirit, speaking in and through Scripture, calls The Presbyterian Church in Canada to confession. This confession is our response to the word of God. We understand our mission and ministry in new ways, in part because of the testimony of Aboriginal peoples.

- We, the 120th General Assembly of The Presbyterian Church in Canada, seeking the guidance of the Spirit of God, and aware of our own sin and shortcomings, are called to speak to the Church we love. We do this, out of new understandings of our past, not out of any sense of being superior to those who have gone before us, nor out of any sense that we would have done things differently in the same context. It is with deep humility and in great sorrow that we come before God and our Aboriginal brothers and sisters with our confession.

- We acknowledge that the stated policy of the Government of Canada was to assimilate Aboriginal

[10] Held in Toronto June 5-10, 1994: Source: https://www.itk.ca/historical-event/presbyterian-church-canadas-residential-schools-apology

peoples to the dominant culture, and that The Presbyterian Church in Canada co-operated in this policy. We acknowledge that the roots of the harm we have done are found in the attitudes and values of western European colonialism, and the assumption that what was not yet moulded in our image was to be discovered and exploited. As part of that policy we, with other churches, encouraged the Government to ban some important spiritual practices through which Aboriginal peoples experienced the presence of the creator God. For the Church's complicity in this policy we ask forgiveness.

- We recognize that there were many members of The Presbyterian Church in Canada who, in good faith, gave unstintingly of themselves in love and compassion for their aboriginal brothers and sisters. We acknowledge their devotion and commend them for their work. We recognize that there were some who, with prophetic insight, were aware of the damage that was being done and protested, but their efforts were thwarted. We acknowledge their insight. For the times we did not support them adequately nor hear their cries for justice, we ask forgiveness.

- We confess that The Presbyterian Church in Canada presumed to know better than Aboriginal peoples what was needed for life. The Church said of our Aboriginal brothers and sisters, "If they could be like us, if they could think like us, talk like us, worship like us, sing like us, work like us, they would know God as we know God and therefore would have life abundant". In our cultural arrogance we have been blind to the ways in which our own understanding of the Gospel has been culturally conditioned, and because of our insensitivity to aboriginal cultures, we have demanded more of Aboriginal peoples than the gospel requires, and have thus misrepresented Jesus Christ who loves all peoples with compassionate, suffering love that all may come to God through him. For the Church's presumption we ask forgiveness.

- We confess that, with the encouragement and assistance of the Government of Canada, The Presbyterian Church in Canada agreed to take the children of Aboriginal peoples from their own homes and place them in Residential Schools. In these schools, children were deprived of their traditional ways, which were replaced with Euro-Canadian customs that were helpful in the process of assimilation. To carry out this process, The Presbyterian Church in Canada used disciplinary practices, which were foreign to Aboriginal peoples, and open to exploitation in physical and psychological punishment beyond any Christian maxim of care and discipline. In a setting of obedience and acquiescence there was opportunity for sexual abuse, and some were so abused. The effect of all this, for Aboriginal peoples, was the loss of cultural identity and the loss of a secure sense of self. For the Church's insensitivity we ask forgiveness.

- We regret that there are those whose lives have been deeply scarred by the effects of the mission and ministry of The Presbyterian Church in Canada. For our Church we ask forgiveness of God. It is our prayer that God, who is merciful, will guide us in compassionate ways towards helping them to heal.

- We ask, also, for forgiveness from Aboriginal peoples. What we have heard we acknowledge. It is our hope that those whom we have wronged with a hurt too deep for telling will accept what we have to say. With God's guidance our Church will seek opportunities to walk with Aboriginal peoples to find healing and wholeness together as God's people.

1998—The United Church of Canada

Rev. Bill Phipps, Moderator[11]

As Moderator of the United Church of Canada, I wish to speak the words that many people have wanted to hear for a very long time. On behalf of the United Church of Canada, I apologize for the pain and suffering that our church's involvement in the Indian Residential School system has caused. We are aware of some of the damage that this cruel and ill-conceived system of assimilation has perpetrated on Canada's First Nations people. For this we are truly and most humbly sorry.

To those individuals who were physically, sexually, and mentally abused as students of the Indian Residential Schools in which the United Church of Canada was involved, I offer you our most sincere apology. You did nothing wrong. You were and are the victims of evil acts that cannot under any circumstances be justified or excused. We know that many within our church will still not understand why each of us must bear the scar, the blame for this horrendous period in Canadian history. But the truth is, we are the bearers of

---

[11] Source: Wikipedia—http://caid.ca/UniChuApo1998.pdf

many blessings from our ancestors, and therefore, we must also bear their burdens.

Our burdens include dishonouring the depths of the struggles of First Nations peoples and the richness of your gifts. We seek God's forgiveness and healing grace as we take steps towards building respectful, compassionate, and loving relationships with First Nations peoples. We are in the midst of a long and painful journey as we reflect on the cries that we did not or would not hear, and how we have behaved as a church. As we travel this difficult road of repentance, reconciliation, and healing, we commit ourselves to work toward ensuring that we will never again use our power as a church to hurt others with attitudes of racial and spiritual superiority.

We pray that you will hear the sincerity of our words today and that you will witness the living out of our apology in our actions in the future.

Appendix III

Selected excerpts from the United Nations Declaration on the Rights of Indigenous Peoples[12]

On September 13, 2007 the United Nations General Assembly adopted Resolution 61/295 affirming:

- That indigenous people are equal to all other peoples, while recognizing the right of all peoples to be different, to consider themselves different, and to be respected as such.

- That all peoples contribute to the diversity and richness of civilization and cultures, which constitute the common heritage of humankind.

---

[12] The complete document available at: www.un.org/esa/socdev/ unpfii/documents/DRIPS_en.pdf

- That all doctrines, policies and practices based on or advocating superiority of peoples or individuals on the basis of national origin or racial, religious, ethnic or cultural differences are racist, scientifically false, legally invalid, morally condemnable and socially unjust.

- Reaffirmed that indigenous peoples, in the exercise of their rights, should be free from discrimination of any kind.

- Recognized that indigenous peoples have suffered from historic injustices as a result of, inter alia, their colonization and dispossession of their lands, territories and resources, thus preventing them from exercising, in particular, their right to development in accordance with their own needs and interests.

- Recognized in particular the right of indigenous families and communities to retain shared responsibility for the upbringing, training, education and the wellbeing of their children, consistent with the rights of the child.

- States are encouraged to comply with and effectively implement all their obligations as they apply to indigenous people under international instruments, in particular those related to human rights, in consultation and cooperation with the peoples concerned.

Article 7

States; that indigenous peoples have the collective right to live in freedom, peace and security as distinct peoples and shall not be subjected to any act of genocide or any other act of violence including forcibly removing children of the group to another group.

Article 10

Indigenous peoples shall not be forcibly removed from their lands or territories. No relocation shall take place without the free, prior and informed consent of the indigenous peoples concerned and after agreement on just and fair compensation and, where possible, with the option of return.

Article 25

Indigenous peoples have the right to maintain and strengthen their distinctive spiritual relationship with their traditionally owned or otherwise occupied and used lands, territories, waters and coastal seas and other resources and to uphold their responsibilities to future generations in this regard.

The Ten Native American Commandments

1. Treat the Earth and all that dwell thereon with respect.

2. Remain close to the Great Spirit, in all that you do.

3. Show great respect for your fellow beings.

4. To work together for the benefit of all Mankind.

5. Give assistance and kindness wherever needed.

6. Do what you know to be right.

7. Look after the wellbeing of mind and body.

8. Dedicate a share of your efforts to the greater good.

9. Be truthful and honest at all times.

10. Take full responsibility for your actions.

Discussion Points

1. Historical understanding of the economic, social, cultural, intellectual, and emotional circumstances of racism.
2. What were the causes of forced integration through the Indian Residential School?
3. Analyze cause and consequence (how and why certain conditions and actions led to others) Esther, Bunnie and Stanley all lost contact with their families and culture when they were still children.

   - How are people affected differently by this loss?
   - How might people's lives' evolve had they not had this experience?

4. How to heal physically and emotionally damaged residential school and post generational survivors. What can be done today about the legacy of Indian Residential Schools?

5. What specific things can we do personally? What can we do collectively?

Reflections:

1. Understand that Racism takes many arrangements.
2. Having read this book, attempt to interview residential and post-residential school survivors.

Epigraph

Many Indian Residential School Survivors, their
families, and their communities continue to face
challenges and hardships today as the result of the
tragic Canadian Government policies of forced
integration and assimilation practices exercised
through 150 years of the Indian Residential School
experiment. The legacy of this experience led our
peoples to complete oppression and economic
dependency on the Crown.

Now is the time to challenge and change this Legacy.
The outcome of this challenge will determine whether
our children face a darker tomorrow or one thriving in
greater human harmony with the rest of Canada.

Chief Roger Wesley
Constance Lake First Nation
Constance Lake, Ontario, Canada